T0224264

Enhancing Information Security and Privacy by Combining Biometrics with Cryptography

Synthesis Lectures on Information Security, Privacy, and Trust

Synthesis Lectures on Information Security, Privacy and Trust is composed of 50- to 100-page publications on topics pertaining to all aspects of the theory and practice of Information Security, Privacy and Trust. The scope will largely follow the purview of premier computer security research journals such as ACM Transactions on Information and System Security, IEEE Transactions on Dependable and Secure Computing and Journal of Cryptology, and premier research conferences, such as ACM CCS, ACM SACMAT, ACM AsiaCCS, IEEE Security and Privacy, IEEE Computer Security Foundations, ACSAC, ESORICS, Crypto, EuroCrypt and AsiaCrypt. In addition to the research topics typically covered in such journals and conferences the series also solicits lectures on legal, policy, social, business and economic issues addressed to a technical audience of scientists and engineers. Lectures on significant industry developments by leading practitioners are also solicited.

© Springer Nature Switzerland AG 2022
Reprint of original edition © Morgan & Claypool 2012

All rights reserved. No part of this publication may be reproduced, stored in a retrieval system, or transmitted in any form or by any means—electronic, mechanical, photocopy, recording, or any other except for brief quotations in printed reviews, without the prior permission of the publisher.

Enhancing Information Security and Privacy by Combining Biometrics with Cryptography
Sanjay G. Kanade, Dijana Petrovska-Delacrétaz, and Bernadette Dorizzi

ISBN: 978-3-031-01207-5   paperback
ISBN: 978-3-031-02335-4   ebook

DOI 10.1007/978-3-031-02335-4

A Publication in the Springer series
SYNTHESIS LECTURES ON INFORMATION SECURITY, PRIVACY, AND TRUST

Lecture #3
Series ISSN
Synthesis Lectures on Information Security, Privacy, and Trust
Print 1945-9742   Electronic 1945-9750

Enhancing Information Security and Privacy by Combining Biometrics with Cryptography

Sanjay G. Kanade, Dijana Petrovska-Delacrétaz, and Bernadette Dorizzi
Institut TELECOM: TELECOM SudParis

SYNTHESIS LECTURES ON INFORMATION SECURITY, PRIVACY, AND TRUST #3

ABSTRACT

This book deals with 'crypto-biometrics', a relatively new and multi-disciplinary area of research (started in 1998). Combining biometrics and cryptography provides multiple advantages, such as, revocability, template diversity, better verification accuracy, and generation of cryptographically usable keys that are strongly linked to the user identity. In this text, a thorough review of the subject is provided and then some of the main categories are illustrated with recently proposed systems by the authors.

Beginning with the basics, this text deals with various aspects of crypto-biometrics, including review, cancelable biometrics, cryptographic key generation from biometrics, and crypto-biometric key sharing protocols. Because of the thorough treatment of the topic, this text will be highly beneficial to researchers and industry professionals in information security and privacy.

KEYWORDS

biometrics, cryptography, crypto-biometrics, cancelable biometrics, revocability, cancelability, diversity, template protection, key generation, key regeneration, key sharing, session key generation and sharing, protocols

Contents

Preface

Securing information during its storage and transmission is an important and widely addressed issue. Generally, cryptographic techniques are used for information security. In cryptography, the general idea is to transform the information during a phase called encryption, before being stored or transmitted, based on a secret key. This secret key is required in order to retrieve the information from the transformed data during decryption. These secret keys are generally too long for a user to remember, and therefore, need to be stored somewhere. The drawback of cryptography is that these keys are not strongly linked to the user identity. In order to strengthen the link between the user identity and his cryptographic keys, biometrics is combined with cryptography.

Unfortunately, biometric systems possess problems of their own such as nonrevocability, non-template diversity, and possibility of privacy compromise which should be taken into consideration. Combining biometrics with cryptography in a secure way can eliminate these drawbacks. Thus, biometrics and cryptography can complement each other. The systems, in which, techniques from biometrics and cryptography are combined are called as crypto-biometric systems. The combined system can inherit the positive aspects of the two while eliminating their limitations.

This is a relatively new domain in which the research started in 1998 and lacks a uniform nomenclature/classification. Therefore, first we present a through and systematic review of crypto-biometric systems. The primary criterion for the classification is the main goal of the system. There can be two principal goals: (i) protecting biometric data, and (ii) obtaining cryptographic keys from biometrics. The systems in these two categories are further divided according to their working methodology. We illustrate each of these categories with our recently proposed crypto-biometric systems. We also study the crypto-biometric systems from the application point of view and their actual usability in information security. We present a review of protocols found in literature which deal with crypto-biometric systems. One such protocol, recently proposed by the authors is discussed in details.

The first system we describe is a shuffling based cancelable biometric system. This is a simple shuffling scheme which randomizes the biometric data with the help of a shuffling key. This shuffling scheme: (a) adds revocability to the biometric systems, (b) improves the verification performance (nearly 80% decrease in equal error rate) because it increases the impostor Hamming distance without changing the genuine Hamming distance, (c) adds template diversity, and (d) makes cross-matching impossible and thus protects privacy.

The second system is for obtaining cryptographic keys using biometrics. The shuffling scheme described above is first applied on the biometric data to make it revocable. This data is then used in a fuzzy commitment based key regeneration scheme. The generic scheme is then adapted to two biometric modalities: iris and face. The amount of errors (variability) in the biometric data for these two modalities is different. Therefore, different sets of error correcting codes are used for these modalities in order to cope with the variability of biometric data. The entropy of keys obtained using the iris and face based key regeneration systems are 83 and 112 bits, respectively.

Finally, we address the issue of sharing crypto-bio keys. We describe a protocol to share the crypto-bio keys generated using our key regeneration scheme. The same crypto-bio key is shared in every run of the protocol. In order to have better security, we proposed another novel protocol to generate and share biometrics based session keys. This protocol allows mutual authentication between the two parties - client and the server - without the need of trusted third party certificates. This protocol has a potential to replace existing key sharing protocols. Moreover, it can easily be integrated into existing key sharing protocols in order to have an additional layer of security.

Sanjay G. Kanade, Dijana Petrovska-Delacrétaz, and Bernadette Dorizzi
May 2012

Acknowledgments

Most of the work included in this book was carried out as part of the project BIOTYFUL (BIO-metrics and crypTographY for Fair aUthentication Licensing) which was supported by the French "Agence Nationale de la Recherche" (ANR) (BIOTYFUL project number ANR-06-TCOM-018).

We would like to thank Diane Cerra, the Executive editor at Morgan & Claypool publishers for her help during the initial phase of this book proposal. We also thank Mr. Michael Morgan for his continuous support throughout the publication process. We would also like to thank Dr. C. L. Tondo and his team for suggesting numerous improvements in the text.

Sanjay Kanade would personally like to thank his parents, Ganesh and Mangala, and his wife Kirti, for their constant encouragement and support during the development of this work. He also acknowledges the help of various past and present members of the Intermedia group at the Electronics and Physics Department, Institut Mines-TELECOM, TELECOM SudParis.

Sanjay Ganesh Kanade, Institut Mines-TELECOM, TELECOM SudParis Dijana Petrovska-Delacrétaz, Institut Mines-TELECOM, TELECOM SudParis Bernadette Dorizzi, Institut Mines-TELECOM, TELECOM SudParis

Sanjay G. Kanade, Dijana Petrovska-Delacrétaz, and Bernadette Dorizzi
May 2012

Abbreviations

AES	Advanced Encryption Standard
ANR	Agence Nationale de la Recherche
BCH codes	Bose, Ray-Chaudhuri and Hocquenghem codes
BIOTYFUL	BIOmetrics and crypTographY for Fair aUthentication Licensing
CBS	Casia BioSecure Database
ECC	Error Correcting Codes
EER	Equal Error Rate
FAR	False Acceptance Rate
FeaLingECc	*Fea*ture *L*evel *F*usion through *W*eighted *E*rror *C*orrection
FRGC	Face Recognition Grand Challenge
FRGC-Exp1*	FRGC Experiment-1 (controlled vs controlled) on our subset
FRGC-Exp4*	FRGC Experiment-4 (controlled vs uncontrolled) on our subset
FRR	False Rejection Rate
GAR	Genuine Acceptance Rate
HTTPS	Hypertext Transfer Protocol Secure
ICE	Iris Challenge Evaluation
ICE-Exp1	ICE Experiment-1 (right eye experiment)
ICE-Exp2	ICE Experiment-2 (left eye experiment)
NIST	National Institute of Standards and Technology
OSIRIS	Open Source Iris Recognition System
RS	Reed-Solomon
SudFROG	SudParis Face Recognition System
TLS	Transport Layer Security

Glossary

The most common terms used in crypto-biometrics are defined below:

1. Biometric template – Set of stored biometric features comparable directly to probe biometric features. It is a special case of a biometric reference, where biometric features are stored for the purpose of a comparison.

2. Identifier/authenticator/credential – Information provided by a user which is required to confirm his identity, e.g., password, token, and biometric characteristics.

3. Verification – One to one comparison of the captured biometric sample with a stored biometric template to verify that the individual is who he claims to be. The result of verification is a Yes/No response.

4. Identification – One to many comparison of the captured biometric sample against a biometric database in an attempt to identify an unknown individual. The result of identification is the identity of a user.

5. Authentication – A term generally used synonymously to verification. In this thesis, we make a distinction between verification and authentication. In addition to verifying the identity of a person based on his credentials, a secure session is opened between the two parties (generally a client and a server).

6. Repudiation – A user can willfully share his credentials and later claim that they were stolen.

7. Crypto-biometric system – A system that combines biometrics with cryptography in order to remove one or more drawbacks of either of the two techniques.

8. Crypto-biometrics – The field of study covering the design, development, evaluation, and analysis of crypto-biometric systems. The research in this field can be dated back since 1998.

9. Cancelable biometric template – The transformed data obtained by applying the cancelable transformation on the reference biometric data.

10. Crypto-biometric template – The template stored in a crypto-biometric system.

11. Helper data – A term used for the data stored in a crypto-biometric system which is required for key (re)generation during verification (e.g., locked code, information for binarization, etc).

12. Crypto-bio key – A key obtained from or with the help of biometric data.

13. Session key – A cryptographic key valid only during a single communication session.

14. BioHash – Quantized multiple projections of a biometric feature vector over a randomly generated ortho-normal matrix. The binary string obtained after quantization is denoted as BioHash. The BioHash may contain variability (i.e., Hamming distance ≥ 0).

15. BioHashing – The process of generating BioHash.

16. Hash key – A user specific key assigned to the user which is required to generate the random ortho-normal matrix for BioHashing.

17. Biometric Hash – Similar to a cryptographic hash. The Biometric Hash does not contain variability (i.e., Hamming distance $= 0$).

18. Stolen biometric scenario – Many crypto-biometric systems involve a secret parameter along with the biometric data (e.g., a Hash key in BioHashing). The stolen biometric scenario is a special case when it is assumed that the biometric data for all the subjects is compromised.

19. Stolen key scenario – Many crypto-biometric systems involve a secret parameter along with the biometric data (e.g., a Hash key in BioHashing). The stolen key scenario is a special case when it is assumed that the secret parameter for all the subjects is compromised.

20. Biometric bottle-neck problem – The result of biometric comparison is one-bit (yes/no). When integrating them in secure authentication systems, this can result in a weak link. attackers can replace the biometric recognition module with a Trojan horse which can provide the required result. We define this situation as biometric bottle-neck problem.

21. Verification string – This is a bit-string stored in crypto-biometric systems. At the time of key (re)generation, another verification string is obtained and compared with the stored one. This comparison is with zero tolerance (i.e., Hamming distance $= 0$). Note that, this string is not used in the key (re)generation process.

22. Systematic error correcting code – An error correcting code is said to be systematic in nature if the input to the code is present in its original form in the output.

CHAPTER 1

Introduction

Biometrics and cryptography are two widely used techniques for providing information security. Biometrics is defined as automated recognition of individuals based on their behavioral and biological characteristics. In biometrics, biological or behavioral characteristics, such as, fingerprints, face, iris, signature, voice, gait, etc., are used to establish the identity of a person. These characteristics are strongly associated with the identity, and therefore, biometric recognition provides a strong link between the user's identity and the authenticator. However, with widespread use of biometrics, many security and privacy concerns are being raised about biometrics. Since biometric characteristics are permanently associated with the person, in case of compromise, they cannot be replaced. This lack of revocability is a serious issue for a user authentication system. Moreover, biometric templates originating from the same biometric characteristic stored in different databases are similar. Therefore, biometrics lack diversity and two biometric databases can be cross-linked compromising privacy. Recovery of biometric data, and a possibility of revealing physical conditions from it, is another privacy issue with biometric systems.

Cryptography, on the other hand, deals with protecting information with the help of secret keys. In cryptography, it is understood that the keys are kept secret, i.e., it requires trust. The keys are linked to the user identity by means of passwords or tokens. However, the passwords or tokens are assigned secrets and are not strongly associated with the person's identity. Therefore, these secrets can be stolen or lost and cryptographic techniques cannot detect the theft. The user can also willfully share the secrets with someone else and the other person can access the system. The authentic user can then make a claim of not accessing the system. This act is called as repudiation.

Fortunately, biometrics and cryptography have complementary characteristics and can be combined to design better and more secure systems. Indeed, since the late 1990's, researchers have tried to combine concepts from these two techniques so that a hybrid system can be designed which can eliminate the drawbacks of both these techniques [49]. Such systems are denoted as crypto-biometric systems in this book. The strong association of biometric characteristics with the user's identity can be utilized to provide the trust required in cryptography. Moreover, the cryptographic techniques can be employed to provide protection to the biometric data without compromising privacy.

In recent times, high attention is being given to information security and privacy concerns and in turn to crypto-biometrics. There is also an increased industrial interest in this subject which is evident through research projects such as BIOTYFUL [8] and TURBINE [4]. Industries are also involved in development of products based on crypto-biometric systems. Recently, an ISO standard—ISO/IEC 24745 [68]—was published related to crypto-biometric systems.

Before going into the information of crypto-biometric systems, we first give some more information about biometrics and cryptography in the following sections.

1.1 INTRODUCTION TO BIOMETRICS

1.1.1 BIOMETRICS

Automated recognition of individuals based on their behavioral and biological characteristics is called biometrics. Some examples of biometric characteristics are fingerprint, iris, face (2D, 3D), retina, palm print, hand veins, ear, knuckles, DNA, voice, signature, gait, typing patterns, etc. These characteristics are denoted as biometric traits or modalities. Since the biometric traits are intrinsically bound to the person, they can be used to establish his identity with a high degree of confidence.

A classical biometric system, as shown in Fig. 1.1, involves two distinct phases: enrollment and recognition/comparison. During enrollment, biometric information (such as fingerprint image or voice data) is captured using specific sensors. This information is processed using specifically designed algorithms to obtain pertinent features. These features are used to create a reference biometric template for the user. The features may be represented as a fixed dimension feature vector (e.g., iris code) or a feature set of variable dimension (e.g., fingerprint minutiae).[1] This reference biometric template is required at the time of verification for comparison purposes and hence, the biometric templates for all such registered users are stored in a central template database for further comparisons.

At the time of recognition/comparison, a fresh sample of the biometric measurement is captured and a similar process, up to obtaining pertinent features, is followed. These features are compared with the stored templates.

Typically, biometric systems can operate in two distinctive modes: (a) identification mode—where the system answers the question, "who is the user?"; and (b) verification mode—where the system answers the question, "is the user really who he is claiming to be?" In other words, during identification, the information extracted from the fresh biometric data is compared with all the stored templates and the identity of the person to which the biometric data belongs is determined. In verification, the person who wants to get verified provides his identity along with his biometric data. A one-to-one comparison is carried out between the information extracted from the fresh biometric data and the stored template corresponding to the provided identity and the result of this comparison is either accept or reject.

A central template database is required for an identification system because all the templates are needed during comparison. If a system is intended for verification purpose only, then it is possible to store the reference templates on a personal storage device such as a smart card. In this way, a two-factor (biometric and a smart card) scheme can be designed which provides increased security.

---

[1] In some cases, biometric model, which is a stored function (dependent on the biometric data subject) generated from biometric feature(s), is stored instead of the biometric templates, e.g., Hidden Markov Model. In this case, during comparison, the function is applied to the biometric features of a probe biometric sample to give a comparison score [69].

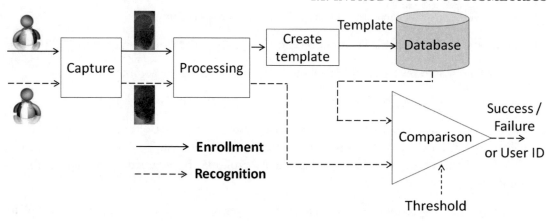

Figure 1.1: Basic idea of a biometric-based person recognition system. In verification mode, the result of the comparison is either success or failure. In identification mode, the result of the comparison is the User ID.

1.1.2   MULTI-BIOMETRICS

An important development in the field of biometrics is to combine information from multiple biometric sources (i.e., cues). A system that consolidates the evidence presented by multiple biometric cues is known as a multi-biometric system. Depending on the sources of information, the multi-biometric system can be referred to as [145]:

- multi-sensor—in which more than one sensors are used to capture information from the presented biometric trait (e.g., capacitive and optical sensors for fingerprints);

- multi-sample—when more than one recording of the biometric trait is used (e.g., multiple face images can be used for creating the template);

- multi-algorithmic—where the same biometric data is processed through multiple algorithms (e.g., minutiae and texture based features for fingerprints);

- multi-unit or multi-instance—in which, multiple instances of the same biometric trait are used (e.g., information from images of left and right irises is combined);

- multi-modal—when more than one biometric traits are used (e.g., a combination of iris and face).

The problem of consolidation of information, presented by multiple biometric sources or cues from any of the types mentioned above, is known as information fusion. The information fusion in a biometric system can be carried out at different levels such as [145]:

- sensor level—information coming from different sensors is combined;

- feature level—the biometric information extracted in form of features is combined;

- score level—match scores of individual biometric comparisons are combined;

- decision level—the results of individual biometric comparisons are combined;

- rank level—when the output of each biometric system is a subset of possible matches (i.e., identities) sorted in decreasing order of confidence, the fusion can be done at the rank level. This is relevant in identification systems where a rank may be assigned to the top matching identities.

Multi-biometric systems offer several advantages over uni-biometric systems, some of which are discussed below.

- Multi-biometric systems can substantially improve the matching accuracy of the system.

- Having multiple information sources increases the size of the feature space available to individual users, thus making it possible to accommodate more individuals in a system.

- Multi-biometrics may address the problem of non-universality, e.g., in a speaker recognition system, the individuals who cannot speak cannot be enrolled. But, inclusion of another biometric such as iris may enable that person to enroll.

- When multiple biometric traits are involved, it becomes more difficult for an impostor to spoof the system.

However, the main disadvantage of multi-biometric systems is their increased complexity.

The biggest advantage of biometrics is that the biometric characteristics are permanently associated with the user. They can neither be stolen nor be shared. Moreover, the biometric characteristics possess permanence—they remain (reasonably) constant throughout the lifetime of the user. Because of the strong association of the biometric traits with the person's identity, they are widely being employed for identity verification. For example, biometric data is included in ePassports. Another example of a large-scale deployment of biometric systems is the US-VISIT (United States Visitor and Immigrant Status Indicator Technology) program in which fingerprints are used for border control [5].

In spite of providing the advantage of a strong link between a person and his identity, biometric systems suffer from some drawbacks. These drawbacks are described in the next subsection.

1.1.3 PROBLEMS ASSOCIATED WITH BIOMETRICS

The biometric characteristics of a person are permanently associated with his identity. Although the property of permanent associativity of biometric data with the user makes biometric systems is useful, it also raises some serious threats. There are two important issues related to biometric systems.

- **Non-revocability:** If the biometric data of a person stored in the database is somehow compromised, it cannot be canceled or replaced. Therefore, the person cannot use the same biometric characteristic in that system and possibly in all other systems based on the same biometric characteristic. This is called non-revocability of biometrics. If it is a fingerprint-based system, the person has an opportunity to use a different finger in that system but still this number of re-enrollments is limited. In case of face, it is not even possible.

- **Privacy compromiser:** With an increasing use of biometric systems, the issue of protecting the privacy of a user is becoming prominent. User privacy is a complicated term. We define three types of privacy compromises.

  1. *Biometric data privacy compromise:* The raw biometric data of the user can be recovered from the stored templates [11, 36, 37, 143]. For example, many fingerprint-based systems use minutiae features and store minutiae extracted from a reference fingerprint image as templates. It is possible to reconstruct the original fingerprint image from the stored minutiae. In some cases, the recovered biometric data can reveal certain biological conditions (e.g., fingerprints can reveal some skin conditions). Additionally, synthesized data can be provided to the system to gain access.

  2. *Information privacy compromise:* When a person enrolls in different biometric systems with the same biometric trait, his templates in all these systems are reasonably similar (provided these systems are based on the same biometric algorithm). Therefore, templates from one database can be used to gain access to another system, and thus, the information stored in that system can be compromised.

  3. *Identity privacy compromise:* Since the templates stored in different databases of a user are reasonably similar, that person can be tracked from one system to another by cross-matching his templates from the two biometric databases. Similarly, when a system operates in identification mode, it can simply reveal that a person, to which the presented biometric belongs to, is enrolled in that particular system. This can be considered as a compromise of user's privacy. For example, consider an application of biometrics to the HIV (Human Immunodeficiency Virus) patients' (or any other sensitive group) social network. This network is a closed group of HIV patients, who share information only to the members. In this scenario, if the biometric recognition system works in identification mode, positive identification of a person based on the provided biometric data indicates that the person is a member of such a sensitive group.

Other than biometrics, most commonly used credentials for establishing user identity can be considered to have one of the following two forms: (1) what you know (i.e., knowledge based, e.g., passwords, pass-phrases, etc.); and (2) what you have (i.e., possession based, e.g., token, smart card, etc.). A user is asked to present one or a combination of these two credentials, and upon their successful verification, access is granted. In such systems, the user identity is established based on the knowledge or possession of an assigned secret. Since these secrets are assigned to the user by the system, they are not intrinsically bound to the user, and hence, can be (more or less) easily stolen. These authenticators can also be shared willfully. Thus, the system based on these two authenticators cannot guarantee the genuineness of the user.

Despite the weak link with the user identity, the knowledge- and possession-based authenticators can be easily revoked. They are assigned secrets, and hence, can be easily changed in case of compromise. Therefore, a combination of biometrics with one of these assigned authenticators can alleviate some of the problems described above. Various cryptographic techniques are used for such a combination. Before we go into the details of combining biometrics and cryptography, a brief introduction to cryptography is provided in the next section.

1.2 INTRODUCTION TO CRYPTOGRAPHY

Cryptography is a process employed widely in order to secure the storage and/or transmission of electronic information. The basic idea of cryptography is shown in Fig. 1.2. It involves two phases: encryption and decryption. During encryption, the data, denoted as *plaintext*, is transformed into unintelligible gibberish, denoted as *ciphertext*, with the help of an encryption key. The decryption process is the reverse of encryption, i.e., obtaining the plaintext from the ciphertext. The pair of algorithms that create the encryption and the reversing decryption is denoted as *cipher*.

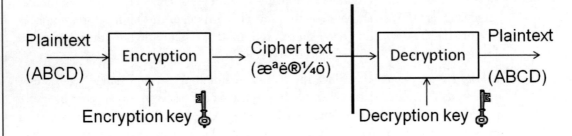

Figure 1.2: Basic idea of cryptography.

1.2.1 SYMMETRIC-KEY AND PUBLIC-KEY CRYPTOGRAPHY

There are basically two types of cryptographic systems: symmetric-key cryptography and public-key (asymmetric) cryptography. In symmetric key cryptographic systems, the encryption and decryption keys need to be the same. Therefore, some other trusted secure mechanism must be employed in order to share the key. Examples of symmetric key cryptography systems include the Data Encryption Standard (DES) and Advanced Encryption Standard (AES) [6].

The advantages of symmetric-key cryptosystems is that they are fast and suitable for real-time applications. Moreover, the security provided by these systems is high as long as the key used for encryption/decryption is secret. However, the symmetric-key cryptosystems require additional key management techniques. The encryption and decryption key used in these systems is the same, and hence, it requires sharing between all the entities participating in the communication. The keys can be shared through other trusted channels, e.g., by registered post or in person. Moreover, if a large amount of data encrypted with a single symmetric key is available, some cryptanalytic attacks can be made easier. Therefore, they need to be frequently renewed.

On the other hand, the public-key cryptographic systems involve a pair of mathematically related cryptographic keys—a public and a private key. The system is designed such that computation of the private key from the public key is computationally infeasible. The public key is accessible to everyone and is used for encryption. The private key, which is required for decryption, must be kept secret. Figure 1.3 shows a diagram of a generic public-key cryptographic system.

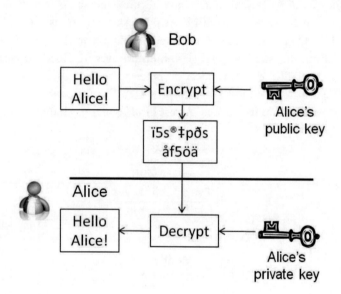

Figure 1.3: Basic idea of public-key (asymmetric) cryptography.

In this figure, there are two entities: Alice and Bob. Bob wants to send a message to Alice in a secure way. Alice has a public-private key pair. She sends the public key to Bob openly. Then Bob encrypts the message with this public key and sends the ciphertext to Alice. The message can be recovered from this ciphertext only with the help of the corresponding private key. Since Alice is the only one having access to this key, only she can recover the plaintext.

Examples of public-key cryptosystems include the Diffie–Hellman key exchange protocol [53], the RSA (Rivest, Shamir, Adleman) algorithm [139], elliptic curve cryptography [90, 115], etc.

The advantage of public-key cryptosystems is that they do not need additional key management techniques. A secure channel is not required for sharing the key since the only shared key is the public key. Unfortunately, the public-key cryptosystems are computationally expensive and hence too slow for practical purposes. Therefore, in practice, hybrid systems are employed in which a symmetric key is shared with the help of a public-key cryptosystem. The symmetric key is used for encryption/decryption in a faster symmetric-key cryptosystem. An example of such a hybrid system is the widely used TLS (Transport Layer Security) protocol [51, 52]. This protocol is used in HTTPS to secure the World Wide Web traffic carried out by HTTP. HTTPS is used for secure e-commerce applications such as online payments through Internet, online banking applications, etc.

Public-key cryptosystems are susceptible to man-in-the-middle attack. In this attack, a cryptanalyst, let's call her Eve, breaks the connection between Alice and Bob. Consider the same situation shown in Fig. 1.3, where Bob wants to send a message to Alice. In this attack (shown in Fig. 1.4), Eve replaces the public key of Alice with her own public key and sends it to Bob pretending to be of Alice. When Bob encrypts the message with Eve's public key and transmits it, Eve can decrypt it with her own private key. Then she can send a malicious message to Alice using Alice's public key. In this way, Alice can think that she is securely communicating with Bob and vice versa, while Eve knows and even can control all the communication between them. A schematic diagram showing the man-in-the-middle attack on a public-key cryptosystem is presented in Fig. 1.4. Note that in the figure the message sent by Bob to Alice is "Arrest him!" which is changed by Eve to "Kill him!"

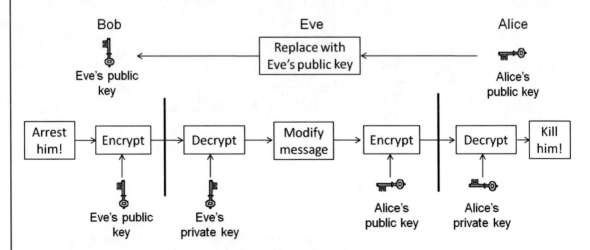

Figure 1.4: Man-in-the-middle attack on a generic public-key cryptosystem. Eve replaces the public key of Alice with her own public key and sending to Bob. Thus, she can access the message sent by Bob. Eve can also modify the text, e.g., here Bob sends the text "Arrest him!" which Eve changes to "Kill him!"

In order to overcome such attacks, various authentication mechanisms are employed in public-key cryptosystems. Nowadays, the most common mechanism is to use trusted third-party certificates which certify the authenticity of public keys. The third party is an entity trusted by all other entities participating in the communication. Some systems also employ password-based authentication. Sometimes, a combination of the two (certificates and passwords) is used. For example, in a typical online banking application the authenticity of the server is confirmed with the help of third-party certificates while that of the user is confirmed based on his secret credentials (password or PIN). Even though the third-party certificates have advantages, this system can work only if the two communicating parties share a common understanding of trust over the third party.

1.2.2   PROBLEMS WITH CRYPTOGRAPHY

According to the Kerckhoffs' principle, the security of a cryptographic system lies entirely on the secrecy of the key [88]. Additionally, for security reasons, the cryptographic keys are required to be long. For example, the possible lengths of keys required in the AES are 128, 192, or 256 bits. For public-key cryptographic systems such as RSA, the key lengths are even higher (e.g., 512, 1024, or 2048 bits). Clearly, a user cannot remember such long keys and therefore, the keys need to be stored somewhere, e.g., on a smart card or in a computer.

In order to restrict access to these keys only to legitimate users, authentication mechanisms are used. Traditionally, authentication mechanisms employed in cryptography are knowledge based (e.g., passwords) or possession based (e.g., token, smart card, etc.). These authenticators are assigned to the user identity and do not necessarily indicate the presence of the person to which they belong. Therefore, they can be (more or less easily) stolen by an attacker, and in this situation, the system cannot distinguish between the attacker and a legitimate user.

Another issue related with these authentication mechanisms is repudiation. A user can willfully share his credentials and later claim that they were stolen. Thus, such a system can be easily cheated.

1.3   INTRODUCTION TO COMBINATION OF BIOMETRICS AND CRYPTOGRAPHY

From the description of problems associated with biometrics and cryptography (Sections 1.1.3 and 1.2.2, respectively), it is clear that both of these techniques need improvements. Biometrics is good at identity verification with better protection against repudiation. Cryptography, which is great in providing security, privacy, and anonymity, requires better verification mechanisms. The common verification mechanisms used in cryptography are based on passwords and/or tokens which are vulnerable due to the weak link between the person's identity and the associated cryptographic keys.

In order to overcome these drawbacks of biometrics and cryptography, over the last decade (since 1998), a new innovative multidisciplinary research field denoted as *crypto-biometrics* has emerged, that combines the two techniques. The systems in which biometrics is combined with cryptography are denoted as *crypto-biometric systems* in this text. With the help of these systems, revocability, privacy, and template diversity can be induced in biometric systems. Also, biometrics-based cryptographic keys, denoted as *crypto-bio keys*, which are strongly linked to the user identity, can be obtained.

The biggest difficulty in combining biometrics and cryptography is that cryptography is precise whereas biometric data contain variability. Cryptography deals with binary keys which need to be exactly the same every time. Unfortunately, biometric data contain some variations in each measurement. Therefore, biometric data cannot be used directly as cryptographic keys, leading to the need to develop specific techniques for designing the crypto-biometric systems.

In this text, we provide a thorough review of the crypto-biometric systems found in literature. Since this field is relatively new (it started in late 1990's), it lacks a uniform classification of the various techniques found in literature. Many researchers call this research field *template protection* and classify these systems as feature transformation and biometric cryptosystems [71, 137]. We would like to point out that template protection is not the only aim of the systems covered in this field. In fact, many systems classified as biometric cryptosystems were originally designed for obtaining cryptographic keys which are strongly linked to the person's identity. Many of these systems do not necessarily meet the criteria for a template protection system (e.g., revocability and privacy protection).

We refer to this research field as *crypto-biometrics* because all these systems combine techniques from biometrics and cryptography. As described in Sections 1.1.3 and 1.2.2, biometrics and cryptography have certain limitations. Crypto-biometric systems attempt to eliminate these limitations by combining the two techniques. Based on their application and functionality, we classify the crypto-biometric systems into two main categories: (a) protection of biometric data and (b) obtaining cryptographic keys with biometrics.

In the first category, cryptographic techniques, such as encryption, hashing, transformation, etc., are used to protect the biometric data. The outcome of these systems is a one-bit verification result similar to the classical biometric systems. On the other hand, in the systems from the second category, biometric data is used to obtain cryptographic keys (denoted as crypto-bio keys). The systems in these two categories are further divided depending on how these techniques are combined. A schematic diagram showing this classification of crypto-biometric systems is shown in Fig. 1.5. Note that the techniques described in these categories can be combined to achieve additional features. A chronological review of the subject can be can be found in [38].

In this text, we discuss systems from each of the two classes of crypto-biometric systems mentioned above. In Chapter 2, a detailed state of the art regarding to the crypto-biometric systems that are designed for protection of biometric data is given. A transformation-based cancelable biometric system recently proposed by the authors is then described along with experimental evaluation on two biometric modalities: iris and face. In Chapter 3, we cover the other category of crypto-biometric systems: obtaining cryptographic keys using biometrics. As it is done in Chapter 2, we first present the state of the art in this category followed by description and experimental evaluation of a key regeneration system proposed by the authors.

Integrating these crypto-biometric systems in secure applications is another challenging problem. Especially for any cryptographic application the cryptographic keys (and in turn, crypto-bio

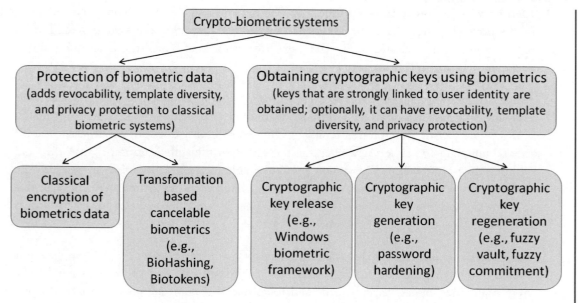

Figure 1.5: The proposed classification of crypto-biometric systems. Primary criterion for this classification is the main goal of the system. Secondary criterion is the methodology used in the system.

keys) need to be shared. There are very few systems that facilitate secure sharing of these crypto-bio keys without the need of conventional public key infrastructure. In Chapter 4, we address this issue. A review of such systems is first presented followed by a discussion of a session-key generation and sharing protocol proposed by the authors.

The systems described in this text were proposed and developed by the authors in the framework of the French "Agence Nationale de la Recherche (ANR)" project BIOTYFUL (which stands for BIOmetrics and crypTographY for Fair aUthentication Licensing), (ANR-06-TCOM-018) [8].

While designing crypto-biometric systems, we set out certain goals for the systems. These goals were defined after studying the state of the art. Additionally, the performance evaluation of these systems is also required to be carried out differently than the classical biometric systems because of the additional cryptographic component. These goals and performance evaluation strategies are discussed in the following sections.

1.4   MOTIVATION AND GOALS

The crypto-biometric systems should be designed in such a way that they inherit the advantages offered by biometrics and cryptography while eliminating their disadvantages. We set the following goals while designing the crypto-biometric systems.

1. **Identity verification and non-repudiation:** The system should be able to confirm the identity of the user with high degree of confidence. It also indicates that the system should resist repudiation attempts carried out by the users. Involvement of biometrics helps achieve this property.

2. **Revocability:** If the stored user template is compromised it should be possible to cancel that template and reissue a new one. Additionally, the newly issued template should not match with the previously compromised template. Thus, revocability does not mean just to cancel the old template and issue a new one; it also means that the authentication rights of the old authenticator are revoked. The system should be able to reject a person if he provides the authenticator linked with the old template. Note that biometrics alone cannot provide this property because biometric characteristics cannot be changed while systems using passwords and tokens have excellent revocability.

3. **Template diversity:** It should be possible to issue different templates for different applications related to the same user. These templates should not match with each other and should make cross-matching impossible. Password- and token-based systems are good at that, although practically, password diversity can be argued. Biometrics, by itself, cannot have template diversity.

4. **Privacy protection:** Crypto-biometric systems should protect privacy. These systems should protect the biometric data privacy, information privacy, and identity privacy, defined in Section 1.1.3.

5. **Performance:** The crypto-biometric system should not degrade the verification performance of the underlying baseline biometric system.

6. **High key entropy:** If the goal of the crypto-biometric system is to obtain crypto-bio keys, the entropy of such keys should be high.

1.5   PERFORMANCE EVALUATION STRATEGIES

In this section, we present the strategy that we followed for performance evaluation of the crypto-biometric systems discussed in this book. The systems that we are going to describe need a biometric system in order to extract features from the biometric data. Additionally, our crypto-biometric systems require the biometric features in binary format. These biometric systems are briefly described in Appendix A. In this work, we relied upon open-source baseline biometric systems. We developed crypto-biometric systems for iris and face modalities. The biometric databases along with their associated experimental protocols are described in Appendix A.

We followed a strategy that the development and evaluation data sets have zero overlap. Different parameters, such as error correction capacities, decision thresholds, etc., are tuned on the development set and with those parameters, the performance is evaluated on the evaluation data sets.

We rely on various metrics to measure the verification performance of the biometric as well as crypto-biometric systems. The performance metrics for biometric systems are discussed in Section 1.5.1, while those for the crypto-biometric systems are discussed in Section 1.5.2. Additional strategies required for security evaluation of the crypto-biometric systems are given in Section 1.5.3.

1.5.1   PERFORMANCE EVALUATION OF BIOMETRIC SYSTEMS

The biometric systems used in this work generate binary feature vectors. The binary feature vectors obtained from the reference and test biometric samples are compared using the Hamming distance. In general, if the two feature vectors are extracted from images belonging to the same person (genuine comparison), the Hamming distance between them is close to zero. On the other hand, if they are from different people (impostor comparison), then the feature vectors are random and differ by a Hamming distance of nearly 0.5. An example of a plot of genuine and impostor Hamming distance distributions is shown in Fig. 1.6.

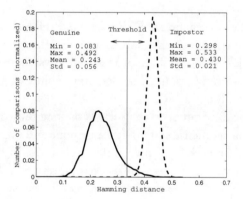

Figure 1.6: An example of Hamming distance distribution plots. The threshold is decided such that the number of genuine Hamming distances above the threshold and the number of impostor Hamming distances below it are minimum.

Comparison of the Hamming distance with a threshold τ leads to an accept/reject decision. There can be two errors in the decision process: *false acceptance* when an impostor is accepted and *false rejection* when a genuine user is rejected by the system. Based on these two errors, the following verification error rates are defined.

- **False Acceptance Rate (FAR):** It is the probability that a non-authorized person is accepted as authorized. It is calculated as a ratio of the number of impostor attempts successfully accepted by the system to the total number of impostor trials.

$$\text{False Acceptance Rate (FAR)} = \frac{\text{Number of impostor attepts accepted}}{\text{Total number impostor trials}}. \qquad (1.1)$$

- **Genuine Acceptance Rate (GAR):** It is the probability that an authorized person is successfully accepted. It is calculated as a ratio of the number of genuine attempts successfully accepted by the system to the total number of genuine trials. It is equal to 1-FRR.

$$\text{Genuine Acceptance Rate (GAR)} = \frac{\text{Number of genuine attepts accepted}}{\text{Total number genuine trials}}. \qquad (1.2)$$

- **False Rejection Rate (FRR):** It is the probability that an authorized person is rejected access. It is the ratio of the number of genuine verification attempts rejected by the system to the total number of genuine trials. It is equal to 1-GAR.

$$\text{False Rejection Rate (FRR)} = \frac{\text{Number of genuine attepts rejected}}{\text{Total number of genuine trials}}. \qquad (1.3)$$

A plot of FRR (or GAR) as a function of FAR is denoted as Receiver Operating Characteristic (ROC) [19]. If the axes of such a plot are on the normal deviate scale, this plot is denoted as Detection Error Trade-off (DET) [112]. The performance of a biometric system can also be summarized with a single number, denoted as operating point. The operating point where the FAR is equal to the FRR is denoted as Equal Error Rate (EER).

The Hamming distance distribution plots (such as the one shown in Fig. 1.6) show the user discrimination capability of the biometric system. If the genuine and impostor distributions are well separated, then the threshold can be set in between the two curves. In this case, there will be zero FAR and FRR. If an overlap between the two curves exists, it results in FAR and FRR.

In order to calculate the verification error rates and confidence intervals, we used the BioSecure Performance Evaluation Tool [7, 132]. This tool employs the parametric confidence interval estimation procedure described in Bolle et al. [22]. The tool calculates the values of EER, operating point (FRR at a given value of FAR), along with their 90% confidence intervals from the similarity scores for genuine and impostor comparisons.

1.5.2   PERFORMANCE EVALUATION OF CRYPTO-BIOMETRIC SYSTEMS

In our crypto-biometric systems, the biometric data are combined with a shuffling key which is obtained using a password. The shuffled data is compared using the same matcher used in the classical biometric system. Every user is assigned a unique and secret shuffling key which ideally is known only to the user. For all the tests, the data pair, consisting of biometric data and the shuffling key, acts as a unit. When a user presents his biometric data for verification, he also provides his unique shuffling key. This implies that, in case of genuine users, the key provided during verification is the same as that used during enrollment of that user, while the biometric data may contain intra-user variability. In case of random impostor tests, an impostor provides his biometric data along with his key.

The verification performance of the crypto-biometric system largely depends on the baseline biometric system it is based upon. From the literature review, we found out that there are systems for which the performance degrades, improves, or remains unchanged. Therefore, it is important to study the change in performance of the system when the biometric information is combined with another secret. In general, a verification system that combines biometric information with another assigned secret, should have better performance than the baseline biometric system because the user is required to carry (e.g., a token) or remember (e.g., a password) another authenticator in addition to his biometrics.

In case of cancelable biometric systems, a similarity (or dissimilarity) score is generated and the verification decision is in form of accept/reject. Therefore, the BioSecure Performance Evaluation Tool [7], [132] can be used for estimating the FAR, FRR, and EER values along with the confidence intervals. In case of key (re)generation systems, the system does not yield a score. Therefore, the BioSecure Performance Evaluation Tool cannot be used to calculate the confidence intervals. Other methods, such as making multiple partitions of the evaluation data and using the mean and standard deviation of the performance on these partitions, can be employed in such cases.

Scheidat et al. [148] proposed two measures for calculating verification performance of key generation systems. These measures are Collision Rate and Reproducibility Rate. But in fact, these two measures are just another names for False Acceptance Rate (FAR) and Genuine Acceptance Rate (GAR) applied to the key generation systems. When the hashes (cryptographic keys in this case) generated from biometric samples of two different users are the same, they call it as collision (which is generally denoted as false acceptance). Collision Rate is the ratio of total number of collisions to the total number of such comparisons. Reproducibility rate is the ratio of number of successful hash generation attempts to the number of comparisons. Since these terms have the same meaning as the conventional terms (FAR and GAR), we use the conventional terms.

1.5.3   SECURITY EVALUATION OF CRYPTO-BIOMETRIC SYSTEMS

The crypto-biometric systems are supposed to increase the security, and therefore, it is required to carry out theoretical as well as experimental security analysis of such systems. Since the systems described in this work have two factors: biometric and shuffling key, it is necessary to evaluate the system performance when one of the two factors is compromised. Hence, two security scenarios are considered: stolen biometric when the biometric data for all the users are compromised; and stolen key when the shuffling keys of all the users are compromised. So, in the stolen biometric scenario, we assume that the impostor has the biometric data of the user. The information he does not have is the shuffling key. Hence, he tries to get verified by providing the stolen biometric data along with his shuffling key.

In the stolen key scenario, the assumption is made that the shuffling keys for all the users are known to the impostors. The other factor—biometric data—is assumed to be secret. In this case, the impostor provides his biometric data along with the stolen shuffling key of the claimed identity.

These two security scenarios are two extreme hypothetical situations, assuming compromise of one of the two factors for all the users. Since the secret information in these scenarios is less than that in the ideal case (where both the factors are secret), the performance of the system is bound to degrade. The question we investigate is that whether the performance degrades beyond the baseline biometric system or not.

Moreover, for the crypto-biometric systems which are used to obtain crypto-bio keys, the length of the key does not really indicate the level of security offered by the system. Although the lengths of the keys can be quite high, the entropy significantly reduces due to the redundancy added by the Error Correcting Codes (ECC). A theoretical estimation of the entropy of the key must be carried out by taking into considerations the redundancy added by the ECC. In this work, we estimate the entropy of the crypto-biometric keys against brute force attacks. We followed the entropy estimation methodology given by Hao et al. [65]. In order to estimate entropy with this approach, the number of degrees of freedom in the biometric data which is used in the key regeneration system must be calculated first. It is done as follows:

Let μ and σ be the mean and standard deviation of the binomial distribution fitting the impostor Hamming distance distribution. Then the number of degrees of freedom is estimated to be:

$$N = \mu(1 - \mu)/\sigma^2. \tag{1.4}$$

Hao et al. [65] use sphere packing bound [104] to estimate the number of brute force attempts required to guess the key. It is based on the degrees of freedom and the error correction capacity of the system. Let's consider that the number of degrees of freedom is N and the error correction capacity is e. The fraction of N corresponding to the error correction capacity e is P. Then the number of brute force attempts required is:

$$BF \approx \frac{2^N}{\binom{N}{P}}, \quad \text{and}$$
$$\text{Entropy} \quad H = log_2(BF). \tag{1.5}$$

This method is frequently used, wherever applicable, in the forthcoming chapters.

1.5.4   TEMPLATE DIVERSITY TEST

In order to prove that a cancelable biometric system adds template diversity, we propose a specific test. In this test, one biometric feature vector is transformed with 100,001 (or even more) transformation parameters. This results in 100,001 different templates from a single feature vector. The first such cancelable template is compared with the remaining 100,000 cancelable templates.

If the Hamming distance (or whichever distance is applicable) distribution of these comparisons is close to the impostor Hamming distance distribution, it indicates that a large number of independent templates can be obtained from a single biometric feature vector using the cancelable biometric system in consideration.

CHAPTER 2

Cancelable Biometric System

2.1 INTRODUCTION

With the increasing use of biometrics, more and more concerns are being raised about the privacy of biometric data. In the existing biometric systems that we denote as "classical biometric systems," the information needed for further comparisons, denoted as biometric reference or template, is stored in a database. This information remains substantially similar across databases if the modality and the biometric algorithm are the same, e.g., for minutiae-based fingerprint systems, minutiae sets extracted from the same fingerprint in different systems are similar. If such template is compromised, it is not possible to replace it with a new one because the biometric characteristics (from which this information is extracted) are permanently associated with their owners. In other words, it is not possible to revoke or cancel a template. This phenomenon is called as lack of revocability.

The permanent association of biometric data with the user leads to another problem. Since the templates in all the systems based on the same biometric characteristic and using same biometric algorithms are similar, a compromised template from one biometric database can be used to access information from another system. This can be referred to as cross-matching between databases, and can be considered as a threat to privacy. Moreover, in some cases, the stored information can be used to create a dummy representation of the biometric trait which can be used to access the system [11, 36, 37, 143]. For example, a dummy finger can be constructed from a fingerprint image.

Because of these reasons, the property of cancelability or revocability is becoming a necessity. In order to induce revocability into biometric systems, cryptographic techniques are a good candidate. Many systems that induce these characteristics are proposed in literature. A review of these systems in presented in Section 2.2. In this chapter, we present a simple shuffling scheme to create cancelable templates from biometric data. This scheme was first proposed by the authors in [77] and involves two factors: biometrics and a shuffling key. Because of this additional parameter, the proposed scheme significantly improves the verification performance of the baseline biometric system. A distinct advantage of this scheme is that its performance in stolen key scenario remains equivalent to that of the baseline biometric system.

This chapter is organized as follows. The state of the art in crypto-biometrics regarding the *protection of biometric data* category is presented in Section 2.2. The shuffling-based cancelable biometrics scheme along with its advantages is described in Section 2.3. Verification performance of this scheme is carried out on iris and face modalities. Details about these evaluations are presented in Section 2.4. Section 2.5 sets out conclusions and perspectives.

2.2 PROTECTION OF BIOMETRIC DATA—STATE OF THE ART

The systems in this category use cryptographic techniques to add some of the desired characteristics (such as revocability, privacy protection, etc.) to biometrics-based verification systems.

We divide these systems in two subcategories: (1) systems using classical encryption of biometric data; and (2) systems employing transformation-based cancelable biometrics. These are discussed in the following subsections.

2.2.1 CLASSICAL ENCRYPTION OF BIOMETRIC DATA

The simplest solution is to encrypt the biometric template with a user-specific password before storing it in the database. Classical encryption techniques, such as the Advanced Encryption Standard (AES) [6], can be used for the purpose. The comparison between the reference and test data cannot be performed in encrypted domain. Therefore, it is required to decrypt the data for comparison purposes at the time of verification. Thus, the biometric template is first recovered from the encrypted template and the comparison is carried out. Figure 2.1 shows a schematic diagram of a generic system of this category.

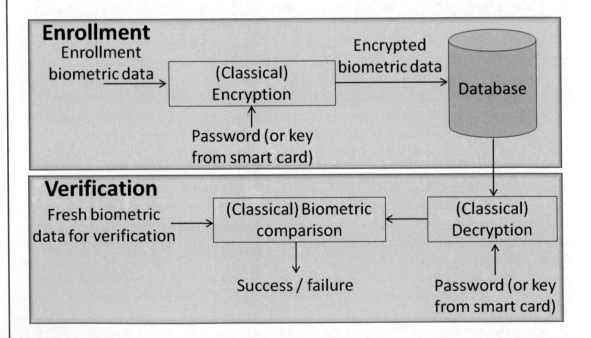

Figure 2.1: Use of classical encryption for protection of biometric data.

Since this system combines biometric information with an assigned secret, in case of compromise, a new template can be issued by changing the password achieving revocability. Moreover, different passwords can be used for different systems to issue different templates, thus achieving template diversity. The security can be enhanced by using a smart card for storing the encrypted template [17].

The drawback of this configuration is that the comparison between a query sample and the targeted template is carried out in a classical way. Therefore, such systems cannot improve the performance of the underlying biometric system. This factor can be seen as a disadvantage from the usability point of view because, in this system, a user is asked to provide password along with his biometric data but there is no performance enhancement. Moreover, once the biometric template is decrypted, it can be misused in different ways (e.g., to obtain the raw biometric data).

2.2.2 TRANSFORMATION BASED CANCELABLE BIOMETRICS

In this category, we group the systems in which the biometric data (raw data such as face image or feature vector such as iris code) is transformed with user-specific transformations. Figure 2.2 shows a schematic diagram of a generic, transformation-based, cancelable biometric system. Note that the transformation applied on the biometric data at the time of enrollment as well as verification is the same. The transformation should be such that the discriminative properties of the original biometric data are preserved in the transformed domain also. This allows the biometric comparison in transformed domain. The user verification decision is taken based on this comparison. The transformation is user specific which is generally controlled using a secret key or password. The transformation acts like an encryption scheme and protects the biometric data. In case of compromise, the transformation parameter (the key or password) can be changed to issue a fresh template, thus achieving revocability. Ideally, this newly issued template does not match with the old template. Similarly, template diversity can be achieved by using different transformation parameters across different systems.

The transformations found in literature are of two types: reversible transformations and irreversible transformations. The reversible transformations make use of a transformation key or token which needs to be kept secret. Such transformations can be inverted to obtain the original biometric data if the transformation key is disclosed. Systems based on these reversible transformation are sometimes called *salting approaches*. The performance of the cancelable systems when using the reversible transformations is generally better than the classical biometric systems. The systems based on irreversible transformations, on the other hand, do not require the transformation parameters to be kept secret. Even if the transformation parameter is disclosed, it is infeasible to obtain the original biometric template from the cancelable template. However, it is observed that the performance of the cancelable biometric systems in such cases degrades compared to the classical biometric systems.

In the following paragraphs, we take a brief look at some of the systems in transformation based cancelable biometrics category. A summary of these systems is presented in Table 2.1.

Table 2.1: Summary of cancelable biometric systems; The verification performances are reported in terms of FAR, FRR, and EER in %.

Ref	Technique	Database	Results	Stolenkey	Remarks
[134, 136]	Various one-way transformations	Proprietary, 188 x 2 fingerprint images	Verification rate 5% less than baseline system	-	-
[74]	BioHashing	Fingerprint, FVC2002-DB1	EER = 0%	-	-
[147]	Cancelable filters	CMU-PIE face	100% verification result; same as baseline	-	-
[161]	BioHashing	FERET face	Better than baseline system	Degrades than baseline system	-
[102]	BioHashing	Fingerprint-FVC2002, face-ORL and Yale-B, signature-SUBCORPUS-100 MCYT	Better than baseline system	Degrades than baseline	-
[58]	Transformation	Proprietary database; 1000 fingerprints	EER = 0%; better than baseline	Same as baseline system	-
[24]	Revocable biotokens	Fingerprints; FVC2000,2,4	Nearly 30% better than baseline	-	-
[105]	Transformation	MCYT signature	EER =13.30%; EER baseline=10.29%	-	-
[110]	Transformation	Proprietary; signature	EER=14%; EER baseline=11%	-	-
–	Shuffling	Iris; NIST-ICE	EER=0.23%; EER baseline=1.71%	Same as baseline system	This work; Chapter 2
[79]	ECC & Shuffling	Iris; NIST-ICE	EER=0.057%; EER baseline=1.71%	Same as baseline system	-
[129]	BioHashing & Bio-Convolving	MCYT signature	EER = 0.36%	4.51%	-

Advantages: Add revocability, template diversity, and privacy protection to biometrics

Limitations: The verification result is one-bit (yes/no). Therefore, they suffer from the biometric bottle-neck problem.

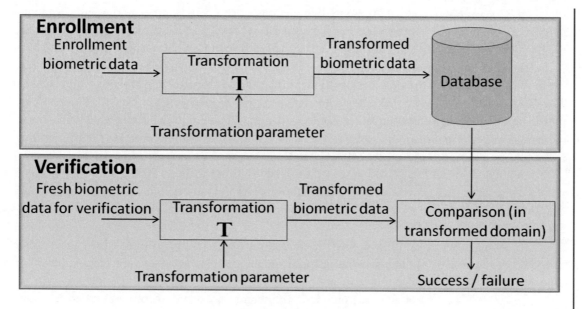

Figure 2.2: Transformation-based cancelable biometrics.

In 2001, Ratha et al. [134] introduced the term cancelable biometrics proposing transformation of the biometric signal (or features) using irreversible transformations. The transformation parameters are user specific. In their recent article, Ratha et al. [135, 136] proposed three different transformations (Cartesian, polar, and functional). These transformations provide a different amount of security to the biometric data. They tested their system on a private database with 188 pairs of fingerprint images and reported that the performance of the underlying biometric system always degrades after transformation.

Another interesting and widely used technique called BioHashing [62] was used by Jin et al. [74] for cancelability.[1] In BioHashing, a randomly generated, user-specific key (denoted as hash key) is used to generate an ortho-normal matrix. The biometric feature vector is projected onto this matrix and after thresholding, a binary vector is obtained which is denoted as BioHash. In 2007, Lumini and Nanni [102] proposed an improved version of this BioHashing scheme with modifications such as binarization threshold variation, space augmentation, feature permutation, and feature normalization. They reported that, in general, BioHashing scheme improves the performance of the underlying biometric system. But, the drawback is, in the stolen key scenario, the performance generally degrades compared to the baseline biometric system.

---

[1]The BioHashing technique was originally proposed for key generation.

In 2006, Teoh et al. [161] presented an analysis of the BioHashing method as a Random Multispace Quantization of the biometric data and the hash key. In their discussion, they argue that the performance degradation in the stolen key scenario is because of the quantization process.

In addition, we would like to comment on the improvement observed in BioHashing. From [74], it is seen that the genuine Hamming distances decrease after application of BioHashing. The same case applies to the stolen key scenario where the same hash key is used for different biometric inputs from impostors and hence decreases the impostor Hamming distances. This results in a decrease in performance in the stolen key scenario. Some other works based on the BioHashing technique are [18, 73, 91, 127, 128, 160, 162, 163].

In 2004, Savvides et al. [147] proposed cancelable biometric filters for face recognition where they use a random kernel (which can be obtained from a PIN) to encrypt facial images. They report that the performance of the baseline biometric system does not change when the transformation is applied.

In 2007, Boult et al. [24] applied the *biotoken* scheme to fingerprints which they earlier proposed for face in [23]. The scheme is based on robust distance matching techniques. They reported 30% improvement in the verification performance for the fingerprint biotoken system.

In 2008, Maiorana et al. [105] proposed a different way of transformation called BioConvolving which is applied to Hidden Markov Model (HMM) based signature features. It makes use of a randomly generated sequence to divide the features into parts on which convolution is applied. In their later papers [107, 110], they showed that the number of different templates that can be generated using this technique is limited and proposed some improvements in order to increase this number. Recently, in [109] they proposed a multi-biometric approach for cancelable biometrics by employing BioConvolving and using a combination of different matchers by score-level fusion.

There is also a proposition by Canuto et al. [35] to use a combination of classifiers with cancelable biometric systems in order to improve the verification performance. Further, Nanni et al. [129] proposed a combination of BioHashing and BioConvolving approaches along with different classifiers for online signatures. They achieved significant improvement in verification performance over the BioConvolving approach.

Recently, in 2011 Ross and Othman [142] proposed using visual cryptography for imparting privacy properties in biometric systems. In this approach, the reference image is dithered into two separate images and stored in two different databases. During matching, both these images are required to reconstruct the reference image which is matched with the query image for biometric verification.

The drawback of many of these cancelable biometric systems is that their performance degrades compared to the baseline biometric system. In some cases, the performance improves, however, the improvement is because of the additional parameter (such as password, PIN, key, token, etc.). Such systems should be analyzed for their verification performance in the stolen key (also called as stolen token) scenario. Such analysis is not reported in most of these works. For BioHashing-based systems, the performance in the stolen key scenario degrades compared to the baseline biometric system.

As opposed to these observations, the performance of the Farooq et al. [58] system in the stolen key scenario remains equal to the performance of the baseline biometric system. This is an important property of this system. The cancelable biometric system that we propose in Chapter 2 possesses this property.

Some other works in the cancelable biometrics category can be found in [12, 13, 42, 43, 46, 98, 99, 165, 186].

2.3   A BIOMETRIC DATA SHUFFLING SCHEME TO CREATE CANCELABLE BIOMETRIC TEMPLATES

The shuffling scheme described in this section was first applied to iris biometrics and then to face biometrics. In general, it can work with any biometric modality provided the biometric features are represented as an ordered set. In this scheme, a randomly generated shuffling key is used to shuffle the biometric data. The shuffled biometric data represents the cancelable template. It is not feasible to recover the original biometric data from this cancelable template. This scheme can be considered analogous to classical symmetric encryption technique because, as in encryption, a key is used to protect the biometric data. But contrary to classical encryption, the user discrimination properties of biometric data are retained by the transformed data, and hence, comparison between two such transformed biometric data can be carried out in the transformed domain. The shuffling technique is explained in details in the next subsection.

2.3.1   THE SHUFFLING TECHNIQUE

The shuffling scheme that we introduce requires a binary shuffling key $\mathbf{K}_{sh}$ of length L_{sh}. Since this key is a long bit-string, it is stored on a secure token or it can be obtained using a password. The biometric feature vector is divided into L_{sh} blocks each of which has the same length. To start the shuffling, these L_{sh} blocks of the feature vector are aligned with the L_{sh} bits of the shuffling key $\mathbf{K}_{sh}$. In the next step, two distinct parts containing biometric features are created: the first part comprises all the blocks corresponding to the positions where the shuffling key bit value is one. All the remaining blocks are taken into the second part. These two parts are concatenated to form the shuffled biometric feature vector which is treated as a revocable template. Figure 2.3 shows a schematic diagram of this shuffling scheme.

The original and shuffled feature vectors have one-to-one correspondence. A block from the original vector is placed at a different position in the shuffled vector. Thus, only the alignment of the feature blocks is changed by the scheme with no change in the actual values of the features. The length of the biometric feature vector does not change because of the shuffling. Hence, the matching algorithms used for calculating the similarity (or dis-similarity) score between two biometric feature vectors are still applicable for the shuffled data.

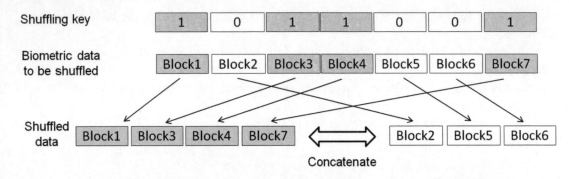

Figure 2.3: The proposed shuffling scheme.

Note that the effectiveness of this scheme is because it changes the alignment of the feature vectors. If the feature vectors do not require any particular order (e.g., fingerprint minutiae sets), this system is ineffective. This system can work only if the biometric data is in form of an ordered set.

2.3.2　ADVANTAGES OF USING THE PROPOSED SHUFFLING SCHEME

The proposed shuffling scheme has the following advantages.

1. **Revocability:** The shuffled feature vector, which is treated as a cancelable template, is a result of combination of an intrinsic identifier (i.e., a biometric characteristic) and an assigned identifier (the shuffling key). Therefore, in case of compromise, it can be canceled and a new template can be generated by changing the shuffling key $\mathbf{K}_{sh}$ (the assigned credential).

2. **Performance improvement:** Another advantage of using the shuffling scheme is that it improves the verification performance. The shuffling process changes the alignment of the feature vector blocks according to the shuffling key. When two biometric feature vectors are shuffled using the same shuffling key, the absolute positions of the feature vector blocks change but this change occurs in the same way for both of the biometric feature vectors. Hence, the Hamming distance (in case of binary vectors) between them does not change. On the other hand, if they are shuffled using two different keys, the result is randomization of the feature vectors and the Hamming distance increases. In fact, the shuffling process acts like a randomizer and moves the average Hamming distance for such cases close to 0.5.

A unique shuffling key is assigned to each subject during enrollment and he has to provide that same key during every subsequent verification. This means, in an ideal case, that the genuine users always provide the correct shuffling key and hence, the Hamming distance for genuine comparisons remain unchanged. On the contrary, in case of random impostor attempts where an impostor tries to get verified with his own credentials, he provides his biometric data along with his shuffling key (or a random shuffling key) to match against other users. The feature vectors for such impostor comparisons are shuffled with two different shuffling keys and the result is that the Hamming distances increase. This effect can be seen in Fig. 2.4. The separation between the genuine and impostor Hamming distance distributions shows the ability of the system to distinguish genuine users from impostors. As can be seen from Fig. 2.4, shuffling increases the separation between the two distributions. In this way, the shuffling scheme improves the verification performance of the system.

3. **Template diversity:** With the help of the shuffling technique, different templates can be issued for different applications by using different shuffling keys with the same biometric data. This particularly helps to avoid cross-database matching. In order to make the template-diversity effective, it is suggested that the shuffling key should be generated randomly and protected by a password.

4. **Protection against stolen biometric data:** If a feature vector is shuffled using two different shuffling keys, the resulting shuffled vectors appear to be originating from two different subjects. They can be seen as comparing two random sequences and hence do not match. Therefore, if a stolen biometric data of a legitimate person is used by an impostor to get verified, the system can still resist such attack due to the use of shuffling key.

5. **Biometric data protection:** It is not computationally feasible to recover the original biometric feature vector from the shuffled data without the proper shuffling key. However, as in classical encryption, the security depends on the secrecy of the shuffling key.

These effects can be better understood from the experimental results and analysis presented in the next section.

2.4   EXPERIMENTAL RESULTS AND SECURITY ANALYSIS OF THE PROPOSED CANCELABLE BIOMETRICS SCHEME

The cancelable biometric system is based upon an underlying baseline biometric system. Therefore, for fair comparison, first the biometric verification performance of the baseline biometric system is reported followed by the performance of the proposed cancelable system.

The proposed cancelable biometric system is evaluated on two biometric modalities: iris and face. For iris, the CBS database [132] is used for development and the NIST-ICE database [131] is used for evaluation purposes. For face, the development and evaluation data sets are derived from the NIST-FRGCv2 database [130]. Details about these databases along with the associated experimental protocols are given in Appendix A. The experimental evaluations of the proposed cancelable system on iris and face modalities are given in the following subsections.

2.4.1   RESULTS AND SECURITY ANALYSIS ON IRIS MODALITY

Experimental Setup

The iris databases and the associated experimental protocols are described in details in Section A.2.1 (page 98).

In case of iris modality, the development database, the CBS database, has two parts: CBS-BiosecureV1 and CBS-CasiaV2. On each of these parts, we carried out 6,000 genuine and 6,000 impostor comparisons. The experimental protocol is designed such that it allows comparisons between images obtained in different sessions and different illumination conditions, and between images of eyes with and without glasses.

The proposed cancelable biometric system is then evaluated on the NIST-ICE iris database. The parameters tuned on the development database (in case of cancelable system, this parameter is the length of the shuffling key) are used for evaluation. The shuffling key is the assigned parameter in the cancelable biometric system which provides protection to the biometric data. Therefore, the length of this key should be long enough from security point of view to avoid brute force attack.

There are two separate experiments defined (and commonly used in the research community) for the NIST-ICE database: ICE-Exp1 consisting of comparisons of right eye images and ICE-Exp2 which consists of left eye image comparisons. All possible comparisons are carried out for genuine as well as impostors. In total, 12,214 genuine and 1,002,386 impostor comparisons are carried out in ICE-Exp1, whereas in ICE-exp2, 14,653 genuine, and 1,151,975 impostor comparisons are performed.

Results on Iris Modality

The genuine and impostor Hamming distance distributions for the CBS-Bio-secureV1 data set before and after shuffling are shown in Fig. 2.4. As described in Section 2.3.2, the shuffling process increases the impostor Hamming distances while the genuine Hamming distances remain unchanged. This can be seen from Fig. 2.4. In this figure, the mean of the impostor Hamming distance distribution of the baseline system shifts from 0.44 to 0.47 when the shuffling scheme is applied. Note that the genuine Hamming distance remains unchanged. This reduces the overlap between the genuine and impostor distribution curves which improves the user discrimination capacity of the system thereby increasing the verification accuracy.

The better separation between genuine and impostor Hamming distance distribution curves improves the verification performance of the system. The verification performance in terms of Equal Error Rate (EER) on the development database (CBS database) is reported in Table 2.2. A clear improvement in performance can be seen by comparing the EER of the baseline system with the proposed cancelable system. For example, on the CBS-BiosecureV1 data set, the EER for the baseline system is 2.63% which reduces to 0.93% when the cancelable scheme is applied. Similarly, on the CBS-CasiaV2 data set, the EER reduces from 3.03% to 0.56% because of the shuffling scheme. For the sake of comparison, the EER values reported in the documentation of the OSIRISv1 on these two data sets are also reported in this table.[2]

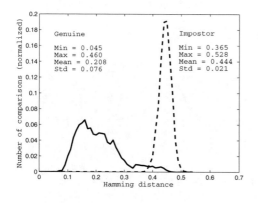

(a) Baseline iris biometric system

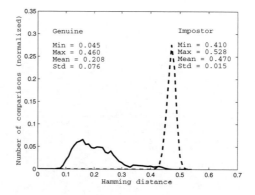

(b) Proposed cancelable biometric system (baseline iris system with shuffling)

Figure 2.4: Normalized Hamming distance distributions for genuine and impostor comparisons on the CBS-BioSecureV1 [132] development data set.

Table 2.2: Verification results of the baseline biometric system (which is based on the OSIRISv1) and the proposed cancelable system on iris modality; development data sets (CBS database [132]); in terms of EER in %. Values in bracket indicate the error margins for 90% confidence intervals.

Experiment	CBS-BiosecureV1	CBS-CasiaV2
Baseline	2.63[±0.34]	3.03[±0.36]
Proposed cancelable	0.93[±0.20]	0.56[±0.16]
OSIRISv1 [132]	2.83[±0.35]	2.12[±0.31]

The proposed shuffling based cancelable biometrics scheme is then evaluated on the NIST-ICE database. As noted before, we carried out separate experiments according to the common protocol for ICE evaluation for right (ICE-Exp1) and left (ICE-Exp2) iris comparisons. The Hamming distance distributions for the ICE-Exp1 experiment are shown in Fig. 2.5.

---

[2]The baseline iris system is based on OSIRISv1; the difference is that the matching module is re-implemented to cope with the iris rotations.

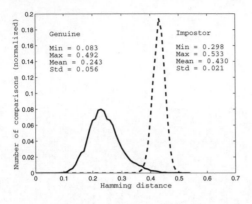

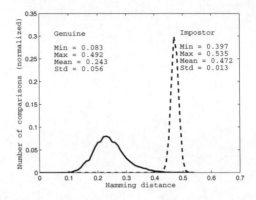

(a) Baseline iris biometric system (ICE-Exp1)

(b) Proposed cancelable biometric system (baseline iris system with shuffling)

Figure 2.5: Normalized Hamming distance distributions for genuine and impostor comparisons on the NIST-ICE [131] evaluation database, for ICE-Exp1 (right-eye experiment).

Similar to the experiments on development sets, a better separation between genuine and impostor Hamming distance curves is seen on the NIST-ICE evaluation data sets. The improvement caused by such change in the Hamming distance distributions is evident from the results given in Table 2.3. The Equal Error Rate (EER) of the system decreases considerably because of the application of shuffling, e.g., on the evaluation database for iris modality, the NIST-ICE database, the EER reduces from 1.71% for the baseline system to 0.23% for the proposed cancelable system for the ICE-Exp1. Similarly, for ICE-Exp2 the EER reduces from 1.80% to 0.37%. Thus, there is nearly 80% reduction in the EER of the cancelable system when compared to the baseline system.

Table 2.3: Verification results of the baseline biometric system (which is based on the OSIRISv1) and the proposed cancelable system on iris modality; evaluation database (NIST-ICE [131]); in terms of EER in %. Values in bracket indicate the error margins for 90% confidence intervals.

Experiment	ICE-Exp1	ICE-Exp2
Baseline	1.71[±0.11]	1.80[±0.10]
Proposed cancelable	0.23[±0.04]	0.37[±0.05]
OSIRISv1 [132]	1.52[±0.12]	1.71[±0.12]

Security Analysis of the Proposed System on Iris Modality

The cancelable biometric system proposed in this chapter has two factors: biometrics and a shuffling key. In order to test the robustness of the system, as described in Section 1.5.3, we carried out the performance evaluation in two extreme hypothetical impostor scenarios: (i) stolen biometric and (ii) stolen key.

In the stolen biometric scenario, we consider a hypothetical extreme situation when the biometric information for all the users is stolen. Here, an impostor will try to provide the stolen biometric data along with a wrong shuffling key. In this situation, the EER increases compared to that of the cancelable system with both factors secret. But, it is still less than the EER of the baseline biometric system. For example, as shown in Table 2.4, for ICE-Exp1 the EER of the cancelable system is 0.23% when both the factors are secret. Considering that the iris image is stolen for all the users, the EER increases to 0.27% which is still less than the EER for baseline system (1.71%). Thus, use of the shuffling scheme prevents the impostors from being successfully verified using stolen biometric data.

Table 2.4: Security analysis of the proposed cancelable system on iris modality in terms of EER in %. Two scenarios are considered: (i) stolen biometric and (ii) stolen key. Values in bracket indicate the error margins for 90% confidence intervals.

Test	Development data set		Evaluation data set	
	CBS-BiosecureV1	CBS-CasiaV2	ICE-Exp1	ICE-Exp2
Baseline	2.63[±0.34]	3.03[±0.36]	1.71[±0.11]	1.80[±0.10]
Cancelable	0.93[±0.20]	0.56[±0.16]	0.23[±0.04]	0.37[±0.05]
Stolen biometric	1.50[±0.26]	0.71[±0.18]	0.27[±0.08]	0.44[±0.09]
Stolen key	2.63[±0.34]	3.03[±0.36]	1.71[±0.11]	1.80[±0.10]

In the stolen key scenario, we consider another extreme situation when the shuffling keys of all the users are compromised. As in the stolen biometric scenario, the EER increases compared to that of the cancelable system having both parameters secret. But, the EER is equal to the EER of the baseline biometric system meaning that the system in this stolen key scenario is still as good as the baseline biometric system (see Table 2.4). In fact, the proposed shuffling scheme is such that it increases the Hamming distance between two iris codes if and only if they are shuffled with different keys. If the same key is used to shuffle two codes, the Hamming distance remains intact. Thus, in the stolen key scenario, the Hamming distance distribution is exactly the same as that for the baseline system, and hence, yields the same result as that of the baseline biometric system. This is a distinct advantage of our system over other cancelable systems found in literature. For most of the cancelable systems found in literature, the performance degrades if the keys (or the cancelable parameters used) are compromised. Only the Farooq et al. [58] system is shown to have the performance equal to the baseline biometric system in the stolen key scenario. See Table 2.1 for a detailed comparison.

Detection Error Tradeoff (DET) curves for the proposed cancelable system along with the security threats are shown in Fig. 2.6 for the iris modality. These curves show the performance on the evaluation database—the NIST-ICE database—for the ICE-Exp1 experiment. The DET curves for the baseline system and that for the stolen key scenario overlap with each other which indicates that the performance of the system in stolen key scenario is same as the baseline system.

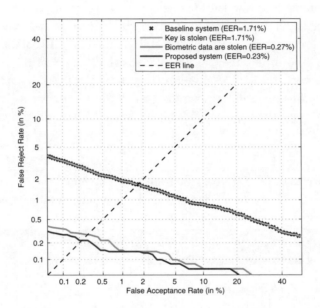

Figure 2.6: DET curves for the proposed system performance along with the possible security threats for iris modality on the NIST-ICE database (evaluation data set) [131]; ICE-Exp1.

The stolen biometric scenario also proves the template diversity concept. It shows that if the biometric feature vector is shuffled with two different keys the two shuffled codes appear to be random. The impostor Hamming distance distributions for the random impostor case (when both, biometric data and key are secret), stolen biometric scenario, and the stolen key scenario are shown in Fig. 2.7 for the iris modality on the NIST-ICE database. Clearly, the distribution for stolen biometric scenario, which is obtained by comparing shuffled iris codes of the same users shuffled with different shuffling keys, lies near the random impostor distribution. This indicates that two iris codes of the same user shuffled using two different shuffling keys, are as different as two shuffled iris codes of two random impostor. Thus, by changing the shuffling key, different templates can be issued for the same user.

We carried out an additional test to prove that the proposed shuffling based cancelable biometric system adds template diversity. We shuffled one iris code with 100,001 randomly generated

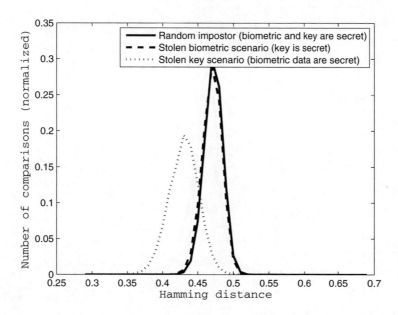

Figure 2.7: Impostor Hamming distance distributions for the proposed system along with the possible security threats for iris modality on the NIST-ICE database [131] (ICE-Exp1).

shuffling keys. The first shuffled iris code is compared with the remaining 100,000 shuffled iris codes. The distribution of Hamming distances obtained from these comparisons is shown in Fig. 2.8. This distribution is also close to the random impostor distribution which validates our claim of template diversity.

In case of compromise, the cancelable template can be revoked. In order to revoke the template, the user is asked to re-enroll into the system. The fresh biometric data is shuffled with a newly generated random shuffling key. Since this shuffling key is different than the one used in earlier enrollment, the old template and the newly issued template cannot match with each other. If an attacker obtains an iris code of the user from previously compromised template or from another biometric system, that iris code cannot be used by the impostor to get verified because the new shuffling key resists such attacks.

2.4.2   RESULTS AND SECURITY ANALYSIS ON FACE MODALITY

Experimental Setup

Details about the data sets used for our experiments on face modality along with the associated experimental protocols are given in Section A.2.2 (page 99).

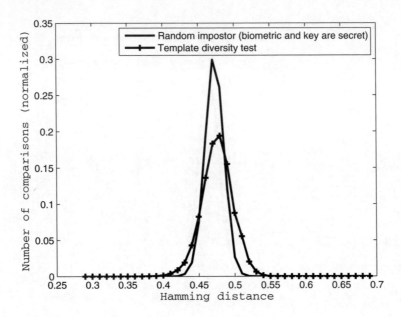

Figure 2.8: Impostor Hamming distance distributions for the proposed system along with the Hamming distance distributions for the template diversity test on iris modality on the NIST-ICE database [131] (ICE-Exp1).

We have derived a subset of the FRGCv2 face database [130] for our experiments. We have used this subset instead of the complete FRGCv2 database in order to reduce the time required to run the full evaluation. The subset used in our experiments is composed of 250 subjects, each of which has 12 images. Data from the first 125 subjects are used for development and the remaining 125 subjects are used for evaluation.

Two separate experiments are carried out during development as well as evaluation: FRGC-Exp1*—where the enrollment as well as test images are captured under controlled conditions, and FRGC-Exp4*—in which the enrollment images are from controlled conditions while the test images are from uncontrolled conditions. For the FRGC-Exp1*, 3,500 genuine and 496,000 impostor comparisons are carried out while for FRGC-exp4*, 4,000 genuine and 496,000 impostor comparisons are performed.

Results

The Hamming distance distribution curves for genuine and impostor comparisons before and after shuffling on the development data sets are shown in Fig. 2.9. The curves for both, FRGC-Exp1* and FRGC-Exp4*, experiments are shown.

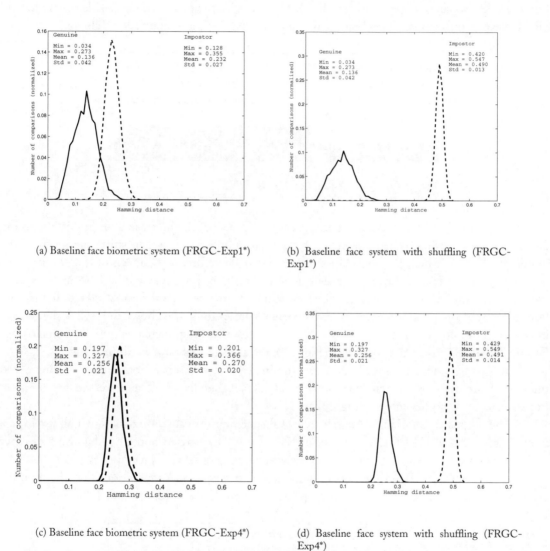

(a) Baseline face biometric system (FRGC-Exp1*)

(b) Baseline face system with shuffling (FRGC-Exp1*)

(c) Baseline face biometric system (FRGC-Exp4*)

(d) Baseline face system with shuffling (FRGC-Exp4*)

Figure 2.9: Normalized Hamming distance distributions for genuine and impostor comparisons on the NIST-FRGCv2 development data set for FRGC-Exp1* and FRGC-Exp4*.

As was observed in case of iris, the impostor Hamming distances increase because of the shuffling process. Note that the genuine Hamming distances remain unchanged. A clear separation between genuine and impostor Hamming distance distributions is observed for both the experiments.

This complete separation results in zero EER. The results of the proposed cancelable system for the FRGC-Exp1* and FRGC-Exp4* on the development data sets are reported in Table 2.5.

Table 2.5: Verification results of the proposed cancelable system on face modality on development data sets in terms of EER in %. The values in bracket indicate confidence intervals.

Test	Development set	
	FRGC-Exp1*	FRGC-Exp4*
Baseline	8.10[±0.41]	35.90[±0.68]
Proposed cancelable	0	0

Note that the improvement in performance is because of the increase in impostor Hamming distances. The shuffling scheme works as a randomization process which shifts the mean of the impostor Hamming distance distribution close to 0.5. Therefore, if the mean of the original (un-shuffled) impostor Hamming distance distribution is small, the improvement in performance will be more prominent. This can be visualized by comparing the improvements for iris and face modalities. For example, on the development data set CBS-BiosecureV1 for iris, as shown in Fig. 2.4, the average impostor Hamming distance for iris is 0.44, which after shuffling, increases to 0.47. Similarly, for face on the development data set Exp1 (Fig. 2.9), the average impostor Hamming distance is 0.23, which moves to 0.49 after shuffling. Thus, the increase in the separation between genuine and impostor Hamming distance curves is more in case of face than for iris. Therefore, the improvement in performance is higher in case of face than in case of iris.

The proposed cancelable system is then evaluated on the evaluation data sets. The two experiments defined earlier, FRGC-Exp1* and FRGC-Exp4*, are carried out. The Hamming distance distributions for these two experiments on the evaluation data sets are given in Fig. 2.10.

As it is seen for the experiments on development sets, a clear separation is obtained on the evaluation sets also. The outcome of this separation is zero EER, as reported in Table 2.6.

Table 2.6: Verification results of the proposed cancelable system on face modality on evaluation data sets in terms of EER in %. The values in bracket indicate confidence intervals.

Test	Evaluation set	
	FRGC-Exp1*	FRGC-Exp4*
Baseline	7.65[±0.40]	35.00[±0.68]
Proposed cancelable	0	0

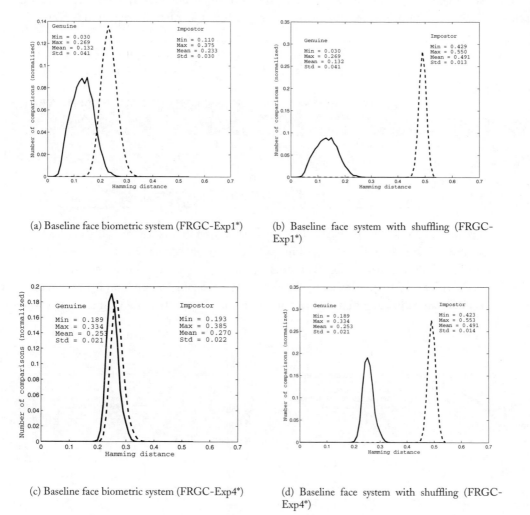

(a) Baseline face biometric system (FRGC-Exp1*)

(b) Baseline face system with shuffling (FRGC-Exp1*)

(c) Baseline face biometric system (FRGC-Exp4*)

(d) Baseline face system with shuffling (FRGC-Exp4*)

Figure 2.10: Normalized Hamming distance distributions for genuine and impostor comparisons on the NIST-FRGCv2 evaluation data set for FRGC-Exp1* and FRGC-Exp4*.

Security Analysis of the Proposed System on Face Modality

The experimental security analysis of the proposed system carried out for the iris modality is performed for the face modality also. The two scenarios—(i) stolen biometric scenario and (ii) stolen key scenario—are followed. During this tests, it is observed that the proposed cancelable system behaves in a similar way as it did on iris. The performance in case of the stolen biometric case remains unchanged. In the stolen key scenario, the performance is exactly the same as that of the baseline biometric system. The results for these tests in terms of EER are reported in Table 2.7.

Table 2.7: Verification results for the cancelable system on face modality in terms of EER in % along with the experimental security analysis. Case-1—face image is stolen; Case-2—shuffling key is stolen.

Test	Development set		Evaluation set	
	FRGC-Exp1*	FRGC-Exp4*	FRGC-Exp1*	FRGC-Exp4*
Baseline	8.10[±0.41]	35.90[±0.68]	7.65[±0.40]	35.00[±0.68]
Proposed cancelable	0	0	0	0
Stolen biometric	0	0	0	0
Stolen key	8.10[±0.41]	35.90[±0.68]	7.65[±0.40]	35.00[±0.68]

As reported in Table 2.7, the EER of the cancelable system on face modality is 0%. Therefore, it cannot be shown using the DET curves. The ROC curves for the face system (evaluation data set) are shown in Fig. 2.11. Similar to the iris modality, the curves for baseline system and that for the stolen key scenario overlap. Moreover, the curves for the cancelable system and the stolen biometric scenario also overlap indicating that the system performance mostly remains unaffected when the face image is stolen.

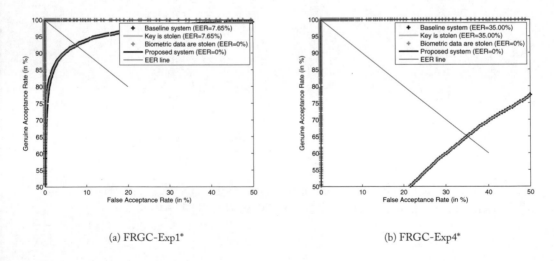

(a) FRGC-Exp1*   (b) FRGC-Exp4*

Figure 2.11: ROC curves for the proposed system performance along with the possible security threats for face modality on the evaluation subset, NIST-FRGCv2 database.

2.5 CONCLUSIONS AND PERSPECTIVES

Classical biometric systems lack the important properties of revocability and template diversity because the biometric traits are permanently associated with the user. Cancelable biometric systems overcome these drawbacks of classical biometric systems. The shuffling scheme described in this chapter employs a randomly generated shuffling key to randomize the biometric feature codes. The shuffled feature vectors act as cancelable templates. The system can issue different templates for different applications using the same biometric characteristic which preserves privacy. If the stored template is compromised, it can be canceled and a new template can be issued by changing the shuffling key. Such use of the shuffling key prevents an attacker from getting verified by providing the compromised template or stolen biometric data. One distinct advantage of this system is that the performance of the baseline system increases by more than 80% due to shuffling. And even if one of the two secret factors, the biometric data and the shuffling key, is compromised, the EER of the system in such scenario still remains less than or equal to that of the baseline biometric system.

The drawback of this shuffling scheme is that it is not noninvertible. Practically, it works as a classical symmetric encryption where data can be encrypted by a key and the encrypted data can be decrypted by providing the same key. If an attacker succeeds to obtain the shuffling key, he can de-shuffle the cancelable template to obtain the reference biometric data. However, when such compromise is detected, the system can revoke the old template and issue a new one and the earlier attack becomes irrelevant.

A limitation of this shuffling scheme in its current form is that it can only be applied to biometric systems when the templates are in form of an ordered set. It cannot be applied to unordered sets such as a set of fingerprint minutiae.

The proposed shuffling scheme is highly effective and therefore it is used as a means to induce revocability in our proposed key regeneration systems in the following chapters.

CHAPTER 3

Cryptographic Key Regeneration Using Biometrics

3.1 INTRODUCTION

In Chapter 1, we classified the crypto-biometric systems in two categories: (a) protection of biometric data, and (b) obtaining cryptographic keys with biometrics. From the first category, we described our earlier proposal of a shuffling based cancelable biometric system in Chapter 2 which add revocability, template diversity, and privacy protection to the classical biometric systems along with improving the verification performance. In this chapter, we first present a detailed literature review of the systems that can obtain crypto-bio keys followed by a through description of our previously proposed crypto-bio key regeneration systems.

Obtaining cryptographic keys using biometrics is a remarkable concept because it offers distinct advantage over classical methods of generating cryptographic keys. Classical cryptographic systems rely on identifiers, such as passwords or tokens, that are assigned to the users by system administrators in order to authenticate the user and generate secure keys for that user. Clearly, these assigned secrets have their own disadvantages like they can be stolen or shared, and hence, are insufficient to prove the user's identity. Using biometrics to obtain cryptographic keys, which are denoted as crypto-bio keys in this text, can provide a better solution as far as identity verification is concerned. The state of the art in this category is described in Section 3.2. Biometrics can be employed for obtaining crypto-bio keys in different ways such as: cryptographic key release, key generation, and key regeneration. The systems described in this chapter are from the third category, i.e., cryptographic key regeneration using biometrics.

From the literature review, it is observed that not many systems achieve all of the goals that we defined for crypto-biometric systems in Section 1.3 (page 9). These goals are: identity verification and non-repudiation, revocability, template diversity, privacy protection, and performance improvement. For most of the systems, the performance gets degraded compared to the baseline system while for those with performance improvement, the performance degrades in the stolen key scenario. Some of the systems do not possess the property of revocability.

The system described in this chapter achieves all these goals. The most important goal of this proposal is to obtain high entropy keys which are strongly linked to the user's identity. The key regeneration system described in this chapter is based on the fuzzy commitment scheme [76]. The fuzzy commitment scheme converts biometric data matching into an error correction problem. Hao et al. [65] proposed an adaptation of this fuzzy commitment scheme for iris biometrics. Their system employs a two-level error correction scheme. Our proposed system is a modified and improved version of this scheme. The shuffling based cancelable biometric system proposed in Chapter 2 is applied on the biometric data before using it in the fuzzy commitment scheme. This makes the system revocable and also improves the verification performance.

As it is done in all fuzzy commitment-based schemes, the proposed system treats the biometric data variability as errors. The system copes with these errors with the help of Error Correcting Codes (ECC). The system described in this chapter is evaluated on two different modalities: iris and face. Since the nature and amount of errors (variability) that can occur in iris are different than that in face, the ECC needs adaptations according to the modality.

This chapter is organized as follows. A detailed state of the art in *Crypto-biometrics: Obtaining Cryptographic Keys with Biometrics* is first given in Section 3.2. A generic proposal for biometric based key regeneration is presented in Section 3.3. One of the most important point to consider while designing this key regeneration system is the selection of ECC. General description about selection of ECC is given in Section 3.3.2. The iris-based key regeneration system along with experimental results is then described in Section 3.4. In Section 3.5, we present another key regeneration system to obtain keys from face biometrics. An extension of the generic scheme in Section 3.3 is presented in Section 3.6. This extended scheme can obtain the reference biometric data and improves the security of the system. Finally, the Section 3.7 sets out our conclusions and perspectives.

3.2   OBTAINING CRYPTOGRAPHIC KEYS WITH BIOMETRICS—STATE OF THE ART

The systems in this category employ biometric recognition techniques to increase the security in a cryptographic framework. Typically, the keys needed for cryptographic applications are obtained using biometric data. These systems are classified in three categories: (a) key release, (b) key generation, and (c) key regeneration, described in following subsections.

3.2.1   CRYPTOGRAPHIC KEY RELEASE BASED ON BIOMETRIC VERIFICATION

The easiest way to integrate biometric systems in a cryptographic framework is to store cryptographic keys securely and release them only after successful biometric verification. Thus, classical biometric user verification is involved in this configuration which provides the verification result and based on which the key (or some parameters required to generate the key) are released. A schematic diagram of this configuration is shown in Fig. 3.1. Note that these systems need to store classical biometric templates as required by the classical biometric system.

An example of this system can be found in Itakura and Tsujii [70] where some secret parameters are released upon successful biometric verification. The released parameters are required to obtain the cryptographic keys.

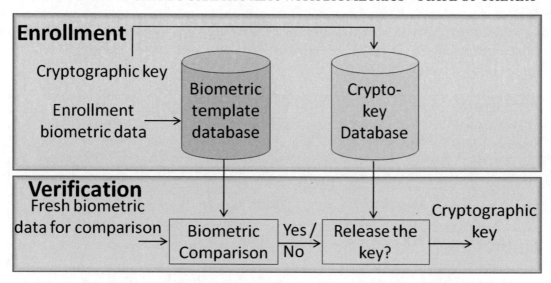

Figure 3.1: Cryptographic key release based on biometrics.

Another example of key release system is the Windows Biometric Framework [113] included in the Microsoft Windows 7. The Windows biometric framework allows users to login to their windows (and other) accounts with their biometric data (currently fingerprints).

The advantage of this approach is its simplicity. There is no need to design specific algorithms for integration of biometrics and cryptography. But, there are few problems associated with this configuration. The biggest and foremost concern is that the biometric template is stored in the system and thus the system inherits all the drawbacks of the biometric system such as non-revocability, non-template diversity, and no privacy protection. These issues can be addressed by employing transformation based cancelable biometric system instead of classical biometric system in this configuration. Another problem is that the verification result of classical as well as the cancelable biometric systems is a single bit information. Therefore, this configuration also suffers from the biometric bottle-neck problem. Because of these shortcomings, the systems in this category cannot achieve the desired enhancement in security. They are mentioned here for the sake of completeness.

3.2.2 CRYPTOGRAPHIC KEY GENERATION FROM BIOMETRICS

From security point of view, a better solution than the key release is to generate a stable bit-string directly from the biometrics. Figure 3.2 shows a schematic diagram of a generic, biometrics based key generation system. These systems are sometimes denoted as template-free biometrics because, in some cases, they do not need storage of templates but they store only the verification string. As shown in Fig. 3.2, the biometric template is not stored in these systems but, only a verification string derived from the biometric data (or from the generated key) is stored. A similar verification string is extracted at the verification time and validity of the key is established by comparing the two verification strings. A summary of the key generation systems is presented in Table 3.1.

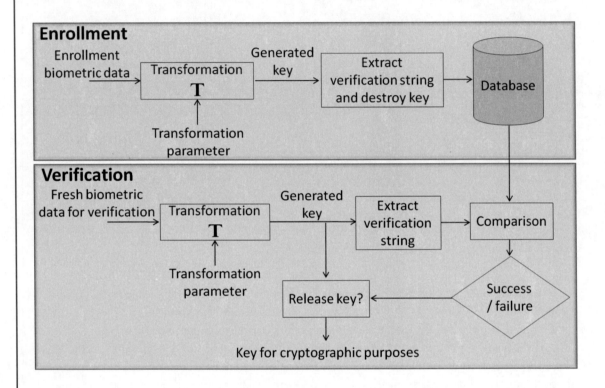

Figure 3.2: Cryptographic key generation using biometrics.

One of the earliest works in this category is that by Davida et al. [49] who proposed an off-line biometric verification scheme. In their proposal, a key is derived from iris data. They proposed using majority coding and Error Correcting Codes (ECC) to stabilize the biometric data. But no experimental results are reported. From our experiments [78] we found out that the majority coding does not work with iris data. Moreover, the assumption in [49] that the Hamming distance between genuine iris codes is 10% is too restrictive.

Another work in this category is the *Hardened password* by Monrose et al. [117]. They combined a typed password with a short string extracted from the user's typing patterns such as durations of keystrokes, and latencies between keystrokes. In a follow-up paper [116], they used voice biometrics instead of keystroke dynamics. They reported increase in entropy from 12 to 46 bits along with a considerable decrease in the FRR.

Table 3.1: Summary of biometrics based cryptographic key generation systems; The verification performances are reported in terms of FAR, FRR, and EER in %.

Ref	Technique	Database	Results	Entropy	Stolenkey	Remarks
[49, 50]	ECC, majority coding	-	Theoretical	-	-	-
[117]	Password hardening	Keystroke dynamics; empirical analysis	FRR = 48.4%	12-bit	-	-
[177]	Statistical features	Online signatures; empirical tests	FAR = 0% at FRR = 7.05%	-	-	Small data set
[62]	BioHashing; Shamir-secret sharing	Spacek's Faces94	Better than baseline system	-	-	-
[116]	Password hardening	Voice; proprietary database	FRR = 20%	46-bit	-	-
[152]	Fuzzy genetic clustering	Signatures; Proprietary database	FRR = 13.1% at 20-bit FAR = 0%	-	-	-
[148]	Biohashing	Online handwriting; proprietary	FRR = 23% at FAR = 2.39%	-	-	Performance degrades than baseline
[14]	ECC	Gait; proprietary database from HUMABIO project and CASIA system	Better than baseline system	-	-	-

Advantages: It can be designed to be template free system, hence no information leakage about the biometric data.

Limitations: Difficult to design, low performance. If no additional parameter (such as password) is used, the system cannot be revocable. The key is not generated randomly.

In 2002, Vielhauer et al. [177] proposed a biometric hash generation scheme based on online signatures. The word hash in "biometric hash" is analogous to the cryptographic hash and should not be confused with the term BioHash proposed in [74]. The biometric hash obtained from the same biometric source is a strictly constant bit-string (i.e., Hamming distance = 0) whereas, the BioHash does contain some variability (i.e., Hamming distance > 0).

The BioPKI system proposed by Hao and Chan [66] can generate private keys using biometrics. But, this system requires storage of classical biometric templates in order to generate the private key. Therefore, it inherits all the drawbacks of the classical biometric systems.

In 2003, Goh and Ngo [62, 164] proposed a random projection based method called Bio-Hashing. An inner product between the biometric feature set and a set of randomly generated vectors is calculated and quantized to obtain a binary string. The random projection space can be obtained from a seed stored on a token. Cryptographic interpolations of Shamir secret shares are then used to obtain a cryptographic key.

Fuzzy genetic clustering is shown to be effective in the work of Sheng et al. [152]. They applied it to handwritten signature data. But, the false rejection rate is quite high (13.1%) for this system. Moreover, the keys have only 20 bits of effective information which is quite low from the security point of view.

In 2009, Argyropoulos et al. [14] used an ECC scheme similar to Davida et al. [49], with a side channel coding approach in which the enrollment biometric data is encoded using a systematic error correcting code.[1] Only the parity symbols of the encoded codeword are stored as a template. At the time of verification, these parity symbols are combined with the test data and decoded to obtain the original enrollment biometric data. Wu et al. [179] applied a similar approach for iris data.

The theoretical construction, called as Helper Data System, proposed by Tuyls and Goseling [168] is a general idea of obtaining biometric based keys. It can be classified as key generation system. Principally, it is similar to the Davida et al. [49] construction. In the helper data system, a secret is extracted directly from the reference biometric data. The helper data is created such that the same secret can be reconstructed with the help of the helper data and a fresh biometric sample.

However, the term helper data is used in general for any auxiliary data stored in the crypto-biometric system which is required for extraction of the secret key during verification. For example, the locked code, which is a combination of a randomly generated secret bound to the reference biometric data, is also called as helper data.

The difficulty of the key generation approach is that the biometric data are not stable. Therefore, it becomes highly difficult to extract a stable string from such data without adversely affecting the verification performance. Scheidat et al. [148] experimentally analyzed the Biometric hash generation algorithm of [177] in both cancelable biometrics and key generation mode. Their study clearly indicates the difficulty of the key generation approach as compared to the cancelable biometrics approach. For a particular test, in cancelable mode, the system has an EER of 3.1% but, for a similar test, the key generation system has an FRR of 23% and an FAR of 2.39%.

---

[1]An ECC is systematic when its output contains the input in original form appended with parity symbols.

Another possible problem with the key generation approach is that the generated key can be considered as a reduced dimensional representation of the biometric data. Hence, unless the system involves some assigned secret (like a seed on a token or a PIN), the keys cannot be revocable.

3.2.3   CRYPTOGRAPHIC KEY REGENERATION USING BIOMETRICS

The most widely studied approach for obtaining keys using biometrics is the key regeneration. Sometimes it is also called key binding [71]. The difference between key generation and key regeneration approach is the way in which the crypto-bio key is obtained. In key generation approach, the key is directly extracted from the biometric data. However, the basic idea behind key regeneration approach is that a randomly generated key is combined with the biometric data using cryptographic techniques and that key is later retrieved from the combined data at the time of verification. A schematic diagram of this approach is shown in Fig. 3.3. The key regeneration systems are summarized in Table 3.2.

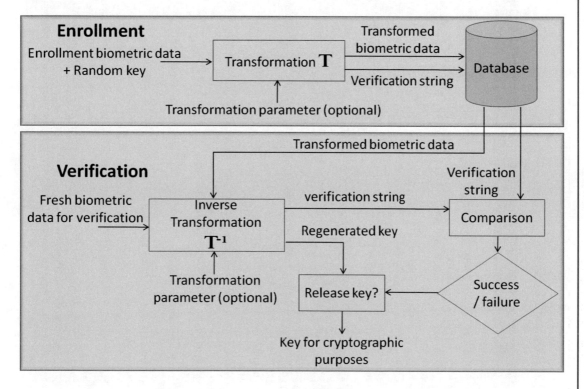

Figure 3.3: Cryptographic key regeneration using biometrics.

One of the earliest works in this approach is by Soutar et al. [154]. They used a signal processing approach to bind the fingerprint data with a random phase-only function. The phase part of the

Table 3.2: Summary of biometrics-based cryptographic key regeneration systems. The verification performances are reported in terms of FAR, FRR, and EER in %.

Ref	Technique	Database	Results	Entropy	Stolen key	Remarks
[76]	Fuzzy commitment	-	Theoretical	-	-	-
[154]	Signal processing	Fingerprints	-	-	-	-
[75]	Fuzzy vault	-	Theoretical	-	-	-
[45]	Fuzzy vault	Fingerprints, empirical study	30% FRR	69-bit	-	-
[54]	Fuzzy extractors	-	Theoretical	-	-	-
[171]	Fuzzy vault	Fingerprints; FVC2002, DB2	20% FRR	-	-	-
[65]	Fuzzy commitment	Iris; proprietary	FRR = 0.47% at FAR = 0%	44-bit	-	Good quality database
[27]	Fuzzy commitment	Iris; NIST-ICE	FRR = 5.62% at FAR = 10^{-5}	-	-	-
[125]	Fuzzy vault	Fingerprints; FVC2002-DB2 [†] and MSU-DBI [‡]	9%[†] and 15%[‡] FRR	-	-	-
[30]	Cancelable and then fuzzy sketch	Fingerprints; FVC2000	FRR = 3% at FAR = 5.53%	-	-	Degraded performance
[122, 124]	Fuzzy commitment and fuzzy vault	Fingerprints (MSU-DBI) and iris (CASIAv1)	FRR = 1.8%	49-bit	-	Our entropy estimate ≈ 23 bits
[119, 121]	Fuzzy commitment and fuzzy vault	FVC2002-DB2	FAR = 0.01% at FRR = 5%	49-bit	-	Our entropy estimate ≈ 36 bits
[108]	User adaptive fuzzy commitment	Online signatures; private database	EER = 17%	-	-	Improved performance
[21]	Key binding using cancelable filters	Face; CMU-PIE database	FRR = 1.4% at FAR = 0%	74 to 103 bits	-	Degraded performance
[77]	Fuzzy commitment and iris shuffling	Iris; NIST-ICE	FRR = 1.04% at FAR = 0.055%	83-bit	FAR = 14.06%	This work; Improved performance
[80]	fuzzy commitment and iris shuffling	Iris; NIST-ICE database	0.18% FRR at 0% FAR; baseline EER = 1.18%	147 bits	FAR=2.98% at FRR=0.27%	Multi-unit system (left and right iris)
[82]	Fuzzy commitment and iris shuffling	Iris NIST-ICE and face NIST-FRGCv2	FRR = 0.91% at FAR = 0% FAR	183 bit	FAR = 36.43%	Multi-biometrics

Advantages: if properly designed, these systems can have the properties of revocability, template diversity, and privacy protection; the keys are randomly generated; high entropy keys can be obtained.

Limitations: The verification performance generally degrades compared to that of the baseline biometric system.

Fourier transform of the fingerprint data is multiplied with the random phase-only function so that the combined data is cryptographically secure. This combined data is then linked with a random cryptographic key using a lookup table. This key is retrieved at the time of verification. Neither the experimental evaluation nor the security analysis of the proposed method are given in [154].

In 1999, Juels and Wattenberg [76] proposed a theoretical scheme called *fuzzy commitment*. A random key is encoded using Error Correcting Codes (ECC) and is then XOR*ed* with the biometric data. The XOR*ed* data is cryptographically secure because neither the key nor the biometric data can be obtained from it without providing one of the two. The random key is retrieved at the time of key regeneration by providing fresh biometric data. This system requires ordered biometric data in binary form.

In 2002, Juels and Sudan [75] developed another theoretical proposal called *fuzzy vault*. The requirement of ordered biometric set of the fuzzy commitment scheme was removed by the fuzzy vault, making it possible to use with biometric modalities such as fingerprints, the minutiae set of which does not have an order. A similar theoretical approach, called fuzzy identity-based encryption, was proposed by Sahai and Waters [146] (in 2005).

In 2004, Dodis et al. [54] introduced the concepts of secure sketches and fuzzy extractors. They provided theoretical security analysis of the crypto-biometric systems which can be applied to the fuzzy commitment and fuzzy vault schemes. Boyen [25] presented a theoretical analysis of the fuzzy extractors and pointed out some of their shortcomings.

Based on these theoretical proposals, many key regeneration schemes are found in literature. Clancy et al. [45] applied the fuzzy vault to fingerprints. They also added some chaff points in the vault to obscure the minutiae. This approach was followed by Uludag and Jain [171] who employed fingerprint orientation-field based helper data along with the vault to improve the performance. But, both these systems have high FRR (30% for [45] and 20% for [171]).

Nandakumar et al. [125] further improved the helper data extraction and fingerprint alignment algorithms presented in [171]. Moreover, they used more than one fingerprint impressions for encoding/decoding. They applied mosaicing technique [144] to combine the minutiae and helper data from two fingerprint impressions which improves the performance. They achieved 30% overall improvement in Genuine Acceptance Rate (GAR=1-FRR) over the system in [171, 172, 173]. But, the GAR is still less than the baseline fingerprint system. Additionally, fingerprint based fuzzy vaults are vulnerable to attacks as described by Scheirer and Boult [151].

Based on the fuzzy commitment proposal, Hao et al. [64, 65] proposed a key regeneration system for iris biometrics. Iris code extracted from an iris image is an ordered set of binary values and thus meets the fuzzy commitment scheme requirements. In order to cope with various errors that can occur in iris data, they proposed a two-level error correction scheme. At first level, Hadamard codes are employed to correct random errors. The Reed-Solomon codes are later used in the second level to correct error bursts that can occur in the iris codes due to eye-lid occlusions, eye-lashes, reflections, etc. Overall error correction capacity of this scheme is 27%. The theoretical security analysis presented in [65] shows that the keys obtained with this system have 44-bit entropy.

Bringer et al. [27, 28] proposed a system similar to [65] with a different ECC scheme: Reed-Muller codes with product codes. The errors in iris codes can contain bursts. In order to break the error bursts in iris data and distribute the errors uniformly throughout the iris code, they employed a random interleaver which increases the error correction efficiency. They obtained 42-bit keys but did not provide any security analysis in terms of entropy.

In the face-based fuzzy sketch of Sutcu et al. [158], user-specific randomization is applied to the biometric feature vectors before processing them through the sketch creation or decoding process. The randomization matrix acts as a user specific secret and thus improves the performance. But, they did not provide analysis considering the compromise of this secret. Moreover, the entropy of the keys is 49-bits.

Maiorana et al. [108] used the fuzzy commitment approach to design their signature based key regeneration scheme. In their proposed approach, they employed adaptive selection of the error correcting codes. In particular, they used BCH codes and selected the parameters of BCH codes adaptively according to intra-user variations. The proposed idea of user adaptive ECC is interesting especially considering the fact that the intra-user variability can vary among different users. The performance shows a little improvement than the baseline biometric system.

There are various template protection schemes in literature that make use of reliable component selection methods to stabilize the biometric data [60, 85, 89, 167, 176, 178, 181, 184]. Basically, these systems, which their respective authors like to call as helper data systems, are fuzzy commitment based schemes. In addition to the commitment, these systems need to store some user-specific helper data required for the reliable bit selection. A critical issue with these systems is that the additional user-specific information can be used for cross-database matching, and may compromise the privacy [87].

Many of these key regeneration systems are based on the fuzzy commitment scheme. However, the requirement of this scheme is that the biometric feature vector needs to be in binary form. Bui et al. [33] proposed a fuzzy commitment based scheme in which an ensemble of quantizers is used. The selection of the quantizer depends on the crypto-biometric key to be bound to the biometric data.

There are also proposals which combine the concepts from cancelable biometrics with key regeneration systems. Such hybrid systems attempt to achieve the advantages of both these classes (i.e., revocability, template diversity, privacy protection along with personal keys). An example of such system is the hardened fuzzy vault by Nandakumar et al. [126]. In this system, they applied a transformation to the biometric features before using them in the fuzzy vault construction.

Bringer et al. [30] also proposed a hybrid scheme for fingerprints. Their scheme applies cancelable transformation to fingerprints and then uses it in a fuzzy sketch. The fuzzy sketch used in this scheme is similar to the one in Bringer et al. [27].

Another example of a hybrid crypto-biometric system is face based template protection system by Feng et al. [59]. In this system, a cancelable transformation is applied on the biometric data followed by a discriminability preserving transform. The binary string obtained after these steps is protected by the fuzzy commitment scheme. The estimated entropy of the keys vary from 203–347 bits.

Boddeti et al. [21] proposed a key binding scheme using correlation filters on face images. They basically extended the correlation filters based cancelable biometric system approach of Savvides et al. [147] to obtain cryptographic keys. A password is used to generate a random kernel which is convolved with face images to make them revocable. The reported entropies, which vary depending on the system parameters, are 74-bits and 103-bits for two different settings.

A drawback of these hybrid systems from the verification performance point of view is that the key generation system performance degrades than the baseline system even though it involves an additional parameter (password or key).

Some other systems in this category can be found in [39, 40, 72, 94, 99, 100, 101, 106, 118, 123, 126, 166, 180, 182, 183, 185]. There are some works related to the security analysis and evaluation of key (re)generation schemes which can be found in [15, 67, 96, 97, 114, 120, 138, 151, 155, 156]. Various attacks against the crypto-biometric systems can be found in these works, including attacks regarding our work (reported in [155, 156]). These attacks are based on the Error Correcting Codes (ECC) output statistics. This attack is briefly explained and solution to counter this attack is presented in Section 3.4.5.

An interesting and emerging development in this research domain is to use multi-biometrics for cryptographic key regeneration. Although there are a large number of multi-biometric systems [140, 141, 145], very few proposals are found in literature which employ multi-biometrics for key regeneration. The reason behind this may be the fact that, in order to obtain high entropy keys, the multi-biometric fusion must be carried out such that the size of the biometric information being used in the crypto-biometric system will increase. In most of the crypto-biometric systems, this biometric information is a set of features (ordered or unordered), and therefore, feature level fusion is a convenient choice. But, the feature level fusion has its own difficulties such as the curse of dimensionality [145] and difference in feature representations of different modalities. The curse of dimensionality imposes limits on the number of features used in a pattern classification system, and hence, it generally needs to be followed by a feature selection process. Score-level fusion, which is a popular way of information fusion in multi-biometric systems, is not possible in key regeneration systems because the reference biometric templates required to calculate individual scores cannot be stored in order to be compliant with the template protection scheme.

Sutcu et al. [157] proposed a method to combine fingerprint and face features in a fuzzy sketch scheme. But, they did not carry out real tests with the fused biometric information but rather predicted the results for the multi-biometric system from the two uni-biometric system results.

In 2008, Nandakumar and Jain [122, 124] proposed a fuzzy vault scheme which combines fingerprints with iris. A significant improvement in verification performance is observed (e.g., from a GAR of 88% and 78.8% for individual iris and fingerprint systems, respectively, to 98.2% for the multi-biometric system). But, the total entropy of the multi-biometric vault (49-bit) is still low. Additionally, the security analysis provided in [122] does not consider the effect of addition of zeros to the iris codes. If zeros are added to the iris code, and error correction is applied to this data, the amount of errors in the biometric data corrected by the ECC is more than the error correction rate of the ECC. In fact, this concept is used in our work (Section 3.4) in order to increase the error correction capacity of Hadamard codes which is otherwise fixed. The increased error correction capacity must be given due attention during estimation of the key entropy. Considering these facts, an analysis of the multi-biometrics based scheme in [122] decreases the entropy from 49 to 23 bits.

In 2008, Cimato et al. [44] proposed a multi-modal biometrics based cryptosystem. Similar to that of Nandakumar and Jain [124], the two modalities employed in their system are iris and fingerprints. Their proposed system is based on the fuzzy extractor concept [25, 54]. They experimentally showed that the performance of the multi-modal system is as good as the best performing single modality system. However, they did not provide security analysis of the system in terms of key entropy.

In 2009, Kelkboom et al. [86] proposed various ways of combining multi-biometrics with fuzzy commitment based schemes. Their proposed systems involve multi-algorithmic fusion at feature-, score-, and decision-level. However, their performance evaluation suggests that the improvement due to multi-biometrics occurs only in terms of verification performance. The security of the system does not improve significantly.

Recently, Fu et al. [61] proposed theoretical models describing multi-biometric cryptosystems. They proposed fusion at the biometric and cryptographic levels and then derived four models adopted at these two levels. However, this work is theoretical and no actual evaluation of verification performance as well as key entropy is carried out.

Combination of different techniques described above can also be employed. For example, Nagar et al. [119, 121] proposed a hybrid crypto-biometric system based on fingerprints. They combined techniques from fuzzy vault and fuzzy commitment in order to make the system more secure and increase the verification performance. Minutiae descriptors, which capture ridge orientation and frequency information in a minutia's neighborhood, are embedded in the vault construction using the fuzzy commitment scheme. Although this system performs better than the fuzzy fingerprint vault scheme [125], a lower performance of the proposed hybrid scheme compared to the baseline fingerprint system is reported.

Table 3.2 presents a summary of key regeneration systems. In the following sections, we describe key regeneration systems that we proposed recently in [77, 84].

3.3 BIOMETRICS-BASED KEY REGENERATION SCHEME

The system described in this section is a hybrid system which combines the ideas from the transformation-based cancelable biometric system (Section 2.2.2) with the biometrics based key regeneration approach (Section 3.2.3). The shuffling based cancelable biometric system described in Chapter 2 is applied on the biometric data before using them in the key regeneration scheme. As said earlier, the key regeneration scheme is an improved version of the Hao et al. [65] scheme which is an adaptation of the fuzzy commitment scheme (which was originally proposed by Juels and Wattenberg [76]) for iris biometrics.

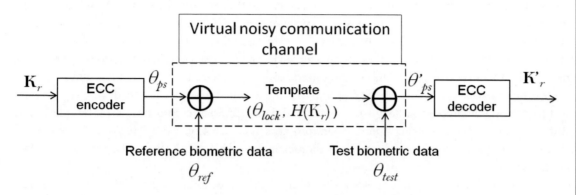

Figure 3.4: A simplified diagram of the fuzzy commitment [76] based key regeneration scheme.

A simplified diagram showing the fuzzy commitment based key regeneration scheme is presented in Fig. 3.4. The fuzzy commitment scheme models biometric data matching as a noisy channel communication problem. A randomly generated key $\mathbf{K}_r$ is treated as the information that needs to be transmitted through the virtual channel which can induce noise in the transmitted data. The noise is caused by the variations in biometric data provided during enrollment and verification. The variations between the reference and test biometric data are treated as errors.

In order to cope with these errors, the key $\mathbf{K}_r$ is first encoded using Error Correcting Codes (ECC) to obtain an encoded codeword θ_{ps} before passing through the virtual channel. The encoded codeword θ_{ps} is called as pseudo-code since its size and nature is similar to that of the biometric data. Bit-wise XOR*ing* is used to combine the reference biometric data θ_{ref} with the pseudo-code θ_{ps}. The XOR*ing* process acts as an encryption algorithm so that neither the key $\mathbf{K}_r$ nor the reference biometric data θ_{ref} can be recovered from the combined data without the presence of either of them. Therefore, the combined data is referred to as locked code θ_{lock}. XOR*ing* the test biometric data θ_{test} with the locked code θ_{lock} transfers the variations between the two biometric data onto the encoded key. The error-transferred encoded key is decoded by the ECC to recover the key $\mathbf{K}'_r$. If the variations between biometric samples are within the error correction capacity of the ECC, the recovered key $\mathbf{K}'_r$ is the same as the original key $\mathbf{K}_r$. In order for the XOR*ing* operation to work, the lengths of the encoded key (i.e., θ_{ps}) and that of the biometric data being XOR*ed* (i.e., θ_{ref} or θ_{test}) must be the same. If they are not, then the biometric data is truncated to match their lengths.

In our proposed scheme, in order to induce revocability, the shuffling based cancelable biometric system described in Chapter 2 is applied on the biometric data before using it in the fuzzy commitment-based scheme. Additionally, we use a two-level error correction scheme first proposed by Hao et al. [65]. The schematic diagram of the proposed system is shown in Fig. 3.5.

3.3.1   REVOCABILITY IN THE KEY REGENERATION SYSTEM

Many systems have been proposed in literature based on the fuzzy commitment scheme described above. One of the most important of these schemes is that proposed by Hao et al. [65] using iris biometrics. Hao et al. [65] proposed a concatenated ECC scheme to cope with the errors (variability) in iris data. In such systems, if it is found out that the original crypto-biometric template is compromised, it can be canceled and a new one can be created by changing the random key K_r. The drawback of this scheme is that the compromised biometric data can still be used to obtain the new crypto-biometric key, since the user is required to provide only the biometric data during verification in this scheme. Moreover, although the system can issue different crypto-biometric templates for different applications by using different random keys K_r, such keys can be recovered from all of them by using a single set of compromised biometric data. This drawback is inherited by the Hao et al. system.

In order for the system to possess the properties of revocability and template diversity, biometric data must be combined with some kind of assigned secret which a user needs to provide at the time of key regeneration. One way to achieve this is by storing the template on a personal smart card. But, this solution limits the job of the attacker (who already has the compromised biometric data) to stealing the smart card. A better solution is to combine the biometric data with a password so that the attacker has to break the password every time the template is revoked. In order to achieve better revocability, we propose a hybrid scheme by modifying the Hao et al. scheme [65]. The cancelable scheme described in Chapter 2 is first applied on the biometric data to induce revocability in the system. Thus, all the advantages of the shuffling scheme as described in Section 2.3.2 are inherited by this key regeneration scheme. A schematic diagram of this proposed system is shown in Fig. 3.5.

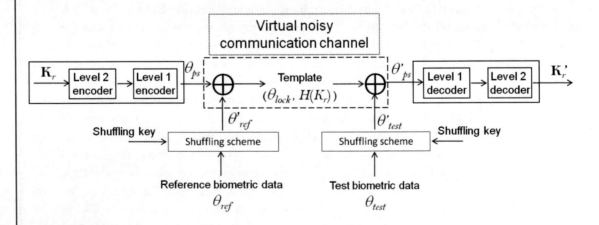

Figure 3.5: The proposed hybrid system for biometrics-based cryptographic key regeneration. It combines the shuffling-based cancelable biometric scheme with the fuzzy commitment-based key regeneration model.

The shuffling scheme in this system can be replaced by another cancelable scheme provided that the error correcting codes are adapted according to the error distribution in the cancelable biometric data. The factors affecting the selection of ECC are described in the next section.

3.3.2   FINDING APPROPRIATE ERROR CORRECTING CODES

The selection of the ECC depends on two criteria: (1) the key $\mathbf{K}_r$ should have a length as big as possible, and (2) ideally, the error correction capacity of the ECC should be such that it can correct *all* of the intra-user variations in the biometric samples. The first criterion indicates that the ECC should have a high code rate. Code rate of an error correcting code is defined as the ratio of the input size to the output size of the ECC. The second condition requires that the error correction capacity is at least as high as the amount of intra-user variations that need to be corrected.

Generally, in order to increase the error correction capacity, the error correcting codes add a large number of parity symbols to the input data which decreases the input data size. These two conditions described above are contradictory and therefore it is particularly difficult to satisfy them simultaneously with a single ECC. Hence, two error correcting codes are used in concatenated mode such that high code rate as well as high error correction capacity is achieved.

As far as biometrics-based key regeneration systems are concerned, this structure was first used by Hao et al. [65] in a fuzzy commitment construct. They used Hadamard codes to correct bit-level errors in the Level-1 whereas, Reed-Solomon (RS) codes were used to correct block-level errors in the Level-2. The selection of these ECC was done related to the errors that occur during different iris acquisitions. Iris data can contain random errors due to camera noise, image distortion, etc., and burst errors caused by eye-lids, eye-lashes, specular reflections, etc. The Hadamard codes correct random errors while the RS codes correct the burst errors. A brief introduction to the Hadamard codes and Reed-Solomon codes is given in the following subsections.

Hadamard Codes

In this section, Hadamard codes are briefly introduced (details can be found in [104]). Hadamard codes are obtained from a Hadamard matrix generated by the Sylvester method. Hadamard matrix is a square orthogonal matrix with elements "1" or "-1". The Hadamard code $HC(k$ is constructed from the Hadamard matrix $H(k)$ as:

$$HC(k) = \begin{bmatrix} H(k) \\ -H(k) \end{bmatrix}. \tag{3.1}$$

The codewords are obtained by replacing -1 with 0 in $HC(k)$. The Hadamard code of size $n = 2^k$ has $2n$ codewords each of which is n bits long. The code has a minimum distance of 2^{k-1} and hence can correct up to $2^{k-2} - 1$ errors (i.e., $\approx 25\%$). During encoding, an input value i is encoded into a codeword w. Here, i is $(k+1)$ bits and w is $n = 2^k$ bits. The matrix $HC(k)$ has $2n$ rows which are considered as codewords. The input value i is considered as a row index and the corresponding row is taken as an output codeword. Thus, an input block of $(k+1)$ bits is converted into an output block of 2^k bits.

At the time of decoding, every 0 in the received codeword w is replaced by -1 to obtain w'. Then the product,

$$w'HC^T(k) = (a_0, a_1, ..., a_r, ..., a_{2n-1}),$$ (3.2)

is calculated. The position r, where a_r is maximum, is the decoded value. If at most $2^{k-2} - 1$ errors have occurred, the decoded value is equal to the input value, i.e., $r = i$.

Reed-Solomon (RS) Codes

Reed-Solomon codes [104] are *nonbinary cyclic* codes with symbols made up of m-bit sequences, where m is any positive integer having a value greater than 2. $RS(n_s, k_s)$ codes on m-bit symbols exist for all n_s and k_s where

$$0 < k_s < n_s < 2^m + 2.$$ (3.3)

Here, k_s is the number of input data symbols being encoded, and n_s is the number of symbols in the output codeword. For the conventional $RS(n_s, k_s)$ code

$$(n_s, k_s) = (2^m - 1, 2^m - 1 - 2t_s),$$ (3.4)

where $2t_s$ is the number of parity symbols and this code can correct at most t_s symbol errors. The RS-codes are systematic codes. An error correcting code is said to be systematic if its output contains the input in original form. In other words, the output of the RS codes, i.e., the n_s symbols is composed of the k_s original data symbols appended with the $2t_s$ parity symbols. More details about Reed-Solomon code can be found in [104, 153].

As mentioned earlier, one of the factors affecting the selection of the ECC is the amount of errors that need to be corrected. This amount is different for different biometric modalities and also different for different experimental conditions, and hence, the ECC need specific adaptations.

In the next section, we propose the specific adaptations of the generalized scheme described above for iris biometrics. The experimental results and security analysis of the proposed system are also presented. Later, the adaptations for face biometrics along with experimental results and security analysis are presented in Section 3.5.

3.4   ADAPTATIONS OF THE PROPOSED GENERALIZED KEY REGENERATION SCHEME FOR IRIS BIOMETRICS

3.4.1   IRIS DATA AND THEIR NOISINESS

As far as the iris data is concerned, the iris codes obtained from the iris images contain two types of errors: random errors caused by camera noise, iris distortion, etc., and burst errors resulting from specular reflections, eyelids occlusions, eyelashes, etc. The random errors are generally distributed over the total size of the iris image. Therefore, when the binary iris code is extracted from such an image, the errors are spread over the whole length of the iris code. On the other hand, burst errors generally occur in a localized manner. Therefore, they are concentrated and result in error burst in iris codes.

Hao et al. [65] proposed a concatenated error correction scheme in which Hadamard codes are used to correct the random errors and RS codes to correct the burst errors. We used the same ECC configuration in our proposed scheme because it suites the nature of errors in the iris data.

The limitation of this ECC configuration is that the Hadamard codes can correct only up to 25% errors. In [65], the authors used a private database having small intra-user Hamming distances. The images in this database are acquired with a camera at a fixed measurement distance from the eye. These acquisition conditions may seem to be too restrictive to the user. As a result of these restrictions, the iris data in this database is far less noisy than in some other publicly available iris databases such as the CBS [132] and the NIST-ICE [131] database. The mean of the genuine Hamming distance distribution for the database in [65] is 0.12 while that for the CBS-BiosecureV1 database is 0.21. Clearly, the database we are working with is much more noisy as compared to the one in [65]. We need to correct nearly 35% errors on our databases. The Hadamard codes having up to 25% error correction capacity are not sufficient to correct these high amount of variations. When we applied the Hao et al. [65] scheme on the CBS-database, the false rejection rate is very high (see Table 3.3, page 60). In fact, the minimum FRR that we could obtain is 13.70% at 0% FAR with 42-bit keys. Bringer et al. [27] also showed that the system in [65], when used on the NIST-ICE database, results in 10% FRR at 0.80% FAR.

Therefore, we propose some adaptations to cope with this high error rate in the following subsection.

3.4.2 ADAPTING THE ECC FROM HAO ET AL. [65] TO CORRECT HIGHER AMOUNT OF ERRORS

A requirement for a biometrics-based verification system is that the genuine users are distinguished from impostors. In fuzzy commitment based schemes, this is achieved by adjusting the error correction capacity. During the development of the proposed iris based system, we used the CBS database [132] in order to find out the optimal error correction capacity for iris data.

By observing the Hamming distance distribution plots for genuine and impostor comparisons on the development data sets (CBS-BiosecureV1) shown in Fig. 2.4 and reproduced here in Fig. 3.6, we found out that the error correction capacity should be set to $\approx 35\%$. In the two-level error correction scheme shown in Fig. 3.5, majority of error correction is performed by the Level-1 codes (Hadamard codes in case of iris) at the background level. Therefore, the FRR can be decreased by increasing the background error correction capacity of Hadamard codes. Hadamard codes can correct only up to 25% errors, and unfortunately, there is no method in literature to alter the error correction capacity of the Hadamard codes. Therefore, we propose a zero insertion scheme which makes it possible to correct more than 25% errors using Hadamard codes. It is achieved by uniformly inserting certain amount of zeros in the iris codes. The zeros are inserted in the iris codes at the enrollment as well as verification time. The positions where the zeros are inserted are fixed and the bits in these locations cannot cause any errors. Therefore, when such iris code is divided into blocks for error correction, each block contains certain amount of zeros and some iris code information bits. Since only the iris code bits can cause errors, the number of errors that can occur in an iris code block decreases. If this amount of errors is less than the error correction capacity of the Hadamard codes, these errors can be corrected.

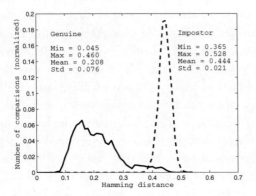 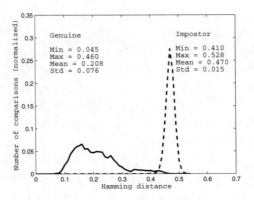

(a) Baseline iris biometric system on CBS-BiosecureV1 (development) data set

(b) Baseline iris system with shuffling on CBS-BiosecureV1 (development) data set

Figure 3.6: Normalized Hamming distance distributions for genuine and impostor comparisons on the development data set (CBS-BioSecureV1) [132]. These plots are the same as shown in Fig. 2.4.

The zero insertion scheme actually alters the error distribution in the iris codes itself by inserting some similarity in both the iris codes to be compared. Inserting similarity does not change the total amount of errors in the comparison data but the amount of errors present per block decreases. Suppose there are p errors in an n-bit block. If q zeros are uniformly inserted in this block, there will be p errors in $(n + q)$ bits. The error ratio decreases from p/n to $p/(n + q)$. If $p/(n + q)$ is less than 25%, then these p errors can now be corrected by the Hadamard codes. The amount of zeros to be inserted is selected such that the error correction capacity matches the requirement (e.g., 35% error correction in our case). The insertion of zeros into the iris code increases its length thereby increasing the number of blocks of Hadamard codes. This allows us to obtain keys of higher length.

The length of the key $\mathbf{K}_r$, denoted by $\| \mathbf{K}_r \|$, depends on the length of the biometric data being XOR*ed* with the pseudo code θ_{ps} and the error correction capability t_s. Thus, increasing the iris code length by zero insertion allows to select longer key $\mathbf{K}_r$.

$$n_s = \frac{\text{Length of biometric data being XOR}ed}{2^{m-1}},$$

(3.5)

$$\| \mathbf{K}_r \| = m \times (n_s - 2t_s). \tag{3.6}$$

Here, n_s is an integer. Hence, the length of the biometric data to be XOR*ed* must be an integer multiple of 2^{m-1}. If it is not, some trailing bits are discarded from the biometric data to match the lengths.

Since the Hadamard codes and RS codes are operating in concatenated mode, their dimensions must also be compatible. Hence, we set the $m = k + 1$ where m is the number of bits in each RS code symbol and k is the order of the Hadamard code. In other words, the size of Hadamard code input is equal to the number of bits in each RS code symbol.

3.4.3 EXPERIMENTAL RESULTS OF THE IRIS-BASED KEY REGENERATION SYSTEM

Experimental Setup

The experimental setup for performing the experiments on iris modality is the same as employed in previous chapters. The databases and associated protocols are detailed in Section A.2.1. The system parameters, mainly the error correction capacity, are tuned on the development database (CBS). The system is further evaluated on the evaluation database (NIST-ICE).

Experimental Results

Before presenting the results of the proposed system, some preliminary results on the development database are presented. Since the proposed system is based on the Hao et al. [65] system, we re-implemented it and tested it on the development database (CBS). The error correction capacity in this system is set at 25%. But, as can be seen from the Hamming distance distribution plots in Fig. 3.6, a significant portion of the genuine Hamming distance distribution curve is present above the 25% Hamming distance mark. This leads to a higher number of false rejections which is evident from Table 3.3. This problem can be solved by allowing a higher number of errors to be corrected.

Table 3.4 shows the results of a modified Hao et al. scheme in which the iris codes are shuffled before using them in the key regeneration framework. A comparison between the Tables 3.3 and 3.4 shows that applying only the shuffling scheme on the iris codes and using them in the Hao et al. scheme does not improve the performance.

The reason for this no-change can be explained as follows: in classical biometric systems, it is observed that at higher values of the verification threshold, the FRR reduces, but at the expense of increase in FAR. As far as the key regeneration system is concerned, the error correction capacity of the error correcting codes used in the system functions as a threshold. If the amount of errors in the iris codes, which is analogous to the Hamming distance, is less than the error correction capacity, the ECC correct those errors and the key is regenerated successfully which is also an indication of successful user verification.

The difference between the experiments reported in Tables 3.3 and 3.4 is only the use of shuffling. The error correction capacity in both these tests is the same. Applying the shuffling

Table 3.3: Results for the Hao et al. [65] system on the CBS database; $n_s = 37$, $m = 6$, effective iris code length=1,184 bits; key length is in bits; FAR and FRR values are in %.

t_s	Key Length	CBS-BiosecureV1		CBS-CasiaV2	
		FAR	FRR	FAR	FRR
1	210	0	77.30	0	97.67
2	198	0	68.05	0	94.95
3	186	0	60.27	0	91.20
4	174	0	53.97	0	86.78
5	162	0	48.28	0	80.67
6	150	0	43.72	0	74.22
7	138	0	38.75	0	67.33
8	126	0	34.45	0	60.57
9	114	0	30.50	0	53.32
10	102	0	26.57	0	46.88
11	90	0	23.18	0	41.30
12	78	0	20.13	0	35.68
13	66	0	17.82	0	31.30
14	54	0	15.25	0	27.02
15	42	0	13.70	0	22.88

scheme increases only the impostor Hamming distances without changing the genuine Hamming distances. Therefore, using a shuffling scheme can decrease the false acceptance rate but the false rejection rate cannot change.

In order to improve the verification performance, the verification threshold, which is the error correction capacity in case of key regeneration system, should be increased. Since the application of the shuffling scheme only increases the impostor Hamming distance, it gives us an opportunity to increase the threshold without increasing the FAR.

The zero insertion scheme described in Section 3.4 is used in order to increase the background error correction capacity. We experimentally determined the amount of zeros to be inserted in the iris codes by performing a number of tests on the development database. One important aspect of the zero insertion scheme is that the zeros should be inserted uniformly throughout the iris code length. At least, there should be roughly equal number of added zeros in each block (to be decoded by Hadamard codes). Considering the fact that the 1,188-bit iris code is obtained by using six filters applied at 198 points of the normalized iris image ($198 \times 6 = 1,188$), we added two zeros after every 3-bit block of the iris code. This increases the length of the iris code from 1,188 bits to 1980 bits. The Hadamard code output is a 32-bit block. Since the increased length of the iris code is not an integer multiple of 32, the iris code is truncated to 1,952-bits by discarding the last 28 bits.

Table 3.4: Results on CBS database: shuffling scheme is applied to the iris codes before using them in the Hao et al. scheme [65]; $n = 37, m = 6$; effective iris code length=1,184; key length is in bits; FAR and FRR values are in %.

t_s	Key Length	BiosecureV1 FAR	BiosecureV1 FRR	CasiaV2 FAR	CasiaV2 FRR
1	210	0	72.5	0	96.6
2	198	0	62.82	0	93.2
3	186	0	55.95	0	88.47
4	174	0	50.53	0	83.18
5	162	0	45.25	0	76.58
6	150	0	40.45	0	70.32
7	138	0	36.37	0	63.65
8	126	0	32.55	0	57.33
9	114	0	28.7	0	50.87
10	102	0	25.47	0	45.5
11	90	0	22.78	0	40.18
12	78	0	20.08	0	35.45
13	66	0	17.3	0	30.65
14	54	0	15.32	0	26.9
15	42	0	13.53	0	23.15

Considering the added zeros, there can be either 20 or 21 actual iris code bits that can cause errors in a 32-bit Hadamard code block. Inherently, this Hadamard code can correct 7-bit errors in a 32-bit block out of which the added zeros cannot cause errors. Thus, the effective maximum error correction capacity is $7/20 = 35\%$.

Table 3.5 shows the detailed results obtained for the proposed iris-based crypto-bio key regeneration scheme on the CBS database. Comparison between Tables 3.3, 3.4, and 3.5 clearly shows the improvement in verification performance as a result of zero insertion and shuffling. For example, using the Hao et al. scheme [65] on CBS-BiosecureV1 data set (Table 3.3), a 198-bit key can be generated with 0% FAR but at an extremely high (68.05%) value of FRR. Adding the shuffling scheme to the Hao et al. scheme also results in similar outcomes (FRR = 62.82%). Clearly, these values of FRR are too high for practical purposes.

But, when the zero insertion scheme is applied along with the shuffling scheme, the FRR decreases drastically without a significant increase in the FAR. For example, a 198-bit key can be obtained with this scheme at FAR = 0.32% and FRR = 3.25% when tested on the CBS-BiosecureV1 database.

Table 3.5: Results for the proposed iris-based key regeneration system on CBS database [132] (development); shuffling is applied on iris codes and 2 zeros added after every 3 bits; $\approx$ 35% error correction; $n_s = 61$, $m = 6$; effective iris code length=1,952; key length is in bits; FAR and FRR values are in %.

t_s	Key Length	CBS-BiosecureV1		CBS-CasiaV2	
		FAR	FRR	FAR	FRR
1	354	0	30.53	0	49.70
2	342	0	22.12	0	35.78
3	330	0	16.37	0	26.27
4	318	0	12.88	0	19.25
5	306	0	10.65	0	14.82
6	294	0	8.98	0	11.70
7	282	0	8.35	0	9.52
8	270	0	7.27	0	7.32
9	258	0	6.60	0	5.97
10	**246**	**0**	**5.87**	**0**	**4.85**
11	234	0	5.28	0.02	3.77
12	222	0.02	4.57	0.08	3.13
13	210	0.03	3.97	0.12	2.12
14	**198**	**0.32**	**3.25**	**0.52**	**1.57**
15	**186**	**0.70**	**2.67**	**1.15**	**1.07**
16	174	1.38	2.00	2.50	0.63
17	162	2.77	1.43	5.30	0.30
18	150	5.55	1.00	9.68	0.25
19	138	9.57	0.63	17.52	0.15
20	126	16.18	0.42	28.20	0.05
21	114	24.42	0.23	41.32	0.03
22	102	36.22	0.13	56.72	0

Using the parameters obtained from the tests on the CBS (development) database (number of zeros to be inserted and values of t_s), the proposed system is tested on the evaluation database—NIST-ICE [131]. These results are reported in Table 3.6.

With the proposed iris-based key regeneration scheme, we succeed to obtain 198-bit keys at 0.055% FAR and 1.04% FRR on the ICE-Exp1 (right eye experiment). For the ICE-Exp2, keys with the same length are obtained at 0.13% FAR and 1.41% FRR. At low FAR range, e.g., FAR=0.0008%, we succeed to obtain 234-bit keys at 2.48% FRR.

Table 3.6: Results for the proposed iris-based key regeneration system on the NIST-ICE database [131]; shuffling is applied on iris codes and 2 zeros added after every 3 bits; $\approx$ 35% error correction; $n_s = 61$, $m = 6$; effective iris code length=1,952; key length is in bits; FAR and FRR values are in %.

t_s	Key Length	ICE-Exp1		ICE-Exp2	
		FAR	FRR	FAR	FRR
1	354	0	49.39	0	52.99
2	342	0	33.26	0	37.74
3	330	0	24.26	0	25.78
4	318	0	16.50	0	20.10
5	306	0	12.67	0	16.25
6	294	0	10.31	0	11.81
7	282	0	7.29	0	9.42
8	270	0	5.93	0.00009	7.77
9	258	0	4.61	0.0002	6.26
10	246	0.0005	3.63	0.0016	4.54
11	**234**	**0.0008**	**2.48**	**0.0022**	**3.49**
12	222	0.0056	2.13	0.033	3.05
13	210	0.021	1.46	0.018	2.12
14	**198**	**0.055**	**1.04**	**0.13**	**1.41**
15	**186**	**0.096**	**0.76**	**0.21**	**1.09**
16	174	0.33	0.69	0.31	0.94
17	162	0.95	0.47	3.14	0.61
18	150	1.81	0.38	5.62	0.46
19	138	11.37	0.26	7.62	0.39
20	126	11.77	0.15	14.77	0.29
21	114	14.20	0.13	18.38	0.20
22	102	21.99	0.11	30.80	0.13

Although the lengths of these keys are quite high, the entropy significantly reduces due to the redundancy added by the ECC. Theoretical analysis of the key entropy is presented in the following subsection.

3.4.4 SECURITY ANALYSIS OF THE IRIS-BASED KEY REGENERATION SYSTEM

In Section 1.5.3, we have defined two ways of security evaluation of the crypto-biometric systems: (i) theoretical analysis to estimate the entropy of the key; and (ii) experimental security analysis for the stolen biometric and stolen key scenarios. This analysis is presented in the following subsections.

Theoretical Security Analysis of the Iris-Based Key Regeneration System
Since the crypto-bio keys obtained using the system described in this section are to be used for cryptographic purposes, it is required to estimate the theoretical entropy of such keys. Originally, the key K_r is randomly generated. But, at the time of regeneration, it is obtained by providing the biometric data along with the shuffling key (or password). Although, ideally, the entropy of the key K_r is equal to its length, the entropy decreases because of the redundancy added by the error correcting codes to cope with the biometric data variations.

As shown in Hao et al. [65], the sphere packing bound [104] can be used to roughly estimate the number of brut force attempts required for an attacker to guess the key K_r correctly. If N is the number of information bits being XOR*ed* with the θ_{ps}, and P is the fraction of this information corresponding to the error correction capacity (i.e., $P = N \times$ error correction capacity), the entropy can be estimated using Equation (3.7) as:

$$H \approx \log_2 \frac{2^N}{\binom{N}{P}} \text{ bits.} \tag{3.7}$$

Although the iris code used in our system is 1,188-bit long, all these bits are not independent but there are some correlations. Daugman [47] described a procedure to estimate the degrees-of-freedom of the iris code based on the statistical data obtained from the impostor comparisons. This procedure takes into account the mean (μ) and standard deviation (σ) of the impostor Hamming distance distribution. Following the same procedure, the degrees-of-freedom in the iris codes can be found as:

$$\text{Degrees-of-freedom } N = \mu(1 - \mu)/\sigma^2. \tag{3.8}$$

There are two approaches an attacker can follow to obtain the cryptographic key: (1) by providing the un-shuffled biometric data and the shuffling key (or password) separately; or (2) by providing the shuffled biometric data.

For the un-shuffled iris data, the average degrees-of-freedom is found to be $N = 556$. If the attacker selects the first approach (which is to provide the iris data and password separately), then using Equation 3.7, the entropy contribution from the iris code is $H_i = 41$-bits. In our scheme, we suggest that the shuffling key should be randomly generated and then protected by using a password. If an 8-character password is generated randomly, it can have up to 52-bit entropy [34]. Therefore, adding this 52-bit entropy of the password to the 41-bit entropy contributed by the iris, the total entropy of the system in this approach is $H_{total} = 41 + 52 = 93$-bits.

If the attacker chooses the second approach (i.e., by directly providing the shuffled data), he needs to guess the shuffled biometric data within a Hamming distance corresponding to the error correction capacity. In this case, the degrees-of-freedom in the shuffled data needs to be calculated. From the experimental data, the mean is found to be $\mu = 0.47$ and the standard deviation is $\sigma = 0.014$. Applying Equation 3.8, the degrees-of-freedom is calculated to be $N = 1,270$. But, there are only 1,172 information bits in the data being XOR*ed*. Therefore, we consider the degrees-of-freedom to be $N = 1,172$. Then using Equation 3.7, the entropy of the system is calculated which is equal to 83-bits.

Thus, theoretically, in case of iris, it is comparatively easier for an attacker to provide the shuffled data directly instead of obtaining the biometric data and shuffling key (or password) separately. Therefore, in summary, the estimated entropy of the keys obtained using the iris-based system is 83 bits.

Experimental Security Analysis of the Iris-Based Key Regeneration System
We carried out the experimental security analysis of the proposed iris-based key regeneration system by conducting two experiments in two extreme scenarios: (a) stolen biometric scenario and (b) stolen key scenario.

In the stolen biometric scenario, it is considered that the impostor has the biometric data for all the genuine users. Therefore, he provides the stolen biometric data along with a random shuffling key. The verification performance (which is actually the false acceptance rate) in this case is reported in Table 3.7.

Table 3.7: Experimental security analysis in terms of FAR (in %) of the proposed iris based crypto-bio key regeneration scheme. Stolen biometric—when iris images of all the genuine users are stolen; key length is in bits; stolen key—when the shuffling keys of all the users are stolen.

t_s	Key Length	ICE-Exp1 Stolen biometric	Stolen key	ICE-Exp2 Stolen biometric	Stolen key
10	246	0	1.66	0	1.32
11	234	0	2.11	0.01	1.64
14	198	0.04	14.06	0.14	12.11
15	186	0.05	23.80	0.06	20.56

In the other extreme security scenario, stolen key scenario, it is assumed that the impostor has obtained the shuffling key for all the genuine users. In this case, the impostor provides his biometric data along with the stolen shuffling key of the genuine user. The false acceptance rate in this scenario is reported in Table 3.7.

The values of FAR in both of these cases are higher than that for the random impostor case when neither biometric nor the key is stolen. If the system does not employ shuffling, the FAR is higher than the FAR in the stolen biometric case and is equal to the FAR in the stolen key scenario. Thus, the use of shuffling prohibits an impostor who has stolen the biometric data while in the stolen key scenario, the system performs as good as the one without using shuffling.

3.4.5   REPORTED ATTACK ON THE IRIS-BASED KEY REGENERATION SYSTEM AND A PROPOSED SOLUTION

Stoianov et al. [155] reported an attack on the proposed key regeneration system using the ECC statistics. In the proposed system, we insert certain amount of zeros at fixed locations in order to increase the error correction capacity of the Hadamard codes. Generally, in a 32-bit Hadamard code block, 12 bits are the added zeros.

Stoianov et al. [155] said:

> "by knowing the locations of only 7 zeros for each 32-bit block, it is possible to reconstruct the entire 198-bit key. For that, the attacker finds the nearest codewords that have the same bits in the known locations (i.e. where the zeros are inserted)."

This attack is possible because the locations of zeros is always fixed and is the same for every user. In order to overcome this attack, we propose a slight modification to the proposed scheme. In the proposed scheme, the iris codes are first shuffled and then zeros are inserted into the shuffled codes. This attack can be avoided if we reverse this process, i.e., if we first add zeros to the iris code and then shuffle it. Since the shuffling key is unique to the user, the locations of the added zeros will be different for each user, thus avoiding the attack.

This attack can also be overcome if the extension of this key regeneration system proposed in Section 3.6 is used. In this extension, the reference biometric data is regenerated in order to obtain constant length keys having higher entropy. This solution involves de-shuffling of the biometric data and can resist the attack described above.

3.5   ADAPTATIONS OF THE PROPOSED GENERALIZED KEY REGENERATION SCHEME FOR FACE BIOMETRICS

3.5.1   FACE DATA AND THEIR NOISINESS

From the study of the key regeneration system on iris modality described in an earlier section, it is clear that the error distribution in the face biometric data should be known, *a priori*, in order to design an error correction scheme for face modality. The amount of variabilities in biometric data changes with the change in experimental conditions and is also different for different modalities.

In Section A.2.2, the face databases and experimental protocols used in this work are explained in detail. We derived a subset of the FRGCv2 face database [130] for our experiments on the face modality. This subset is composed of 250 subjects each of which has 12 images. Data from the first 125 subjects are used for development and the remaining 125 subjects are used for evaluation.

We carried out two separate experiments during development as well as evaluation: FRGC-Exp1*—where the enrollment as well as test images are captured under controlled conditions, and FRGC-Exp4*—in which the enrollment images are from controlled conditions while the test images are from uncontrolled conditions. For the FRGC-Exp1*, 3,500 genuine and 496,000 impostor comparisons are carried out while for FRGC-exp4*, 4,000 genuine and 496,000 impostor comparisons are performed.

These two experiments carried out on the FRGCv2 data set have different characteristics. For the FRGC-Exp1*, in which images from controlled set are compared against those in controlled set, the amount of variations in the face codes is less. Our goal is to correct only the intra-user variations in the face data. Observing the Hamming distance distribution curves for the FRGC-Exp1* face data shown in Fig. 3.7(a), we found out that the amount of intra-user variations that need to be corrected is nearly 21%. Clearly, using Hadamard codes in this case cannot work because Hadamard codes correct nearly 25% errors which is higher than the required capacity. Therefore, we selected BCH codes [104] as Level-1 ECC. For more details about the BCH codes, please refer to [104]. On the contrary, for the FRGC-Exp4* (Fig. 3.7(c)), the intra-user variations are nearly 30%, which is higher than the maximum error correction capacity of BCH as well as Hadamard codes. Therefore, similar to the iris case, we selected Hadamard codes along with zero insertion module to correct those errors.

3.5.2   SELECTING AND ADAPTING ECC TO THE FACE DATA

Observing the Hamming distance distribution plots for the FRGC-Exp1* face data shown in Fig. 3.7(a), we selected BCH(511,28,111) as Level-1 ECC. This code converts an input block of 28 bits into an output block of 511 bits, and this code can correct 111 errors that can occur in the 511 bits. Thus, the error correction capacity of these codes is 21.72%. As described in Section 3.3.2, the goal of using concatenated ECC is to increase the code rate which increases the length of the crypto-bio key. Therefore, the BCH-codes and RS-codes are employed in concatenated fashion and it is required that their dimensions should be compatible with each other.

Ideally, the output block size of the Level-2 codes should be equal to the input block size of the Level-1 codes. Optionally, the Level-1 codes input block size can be an integer multiple of the output block size of the Level-2 codes so that multiple blocks of Level-2 codes can be combined to obtain a Level-1 codes block. For the FRGC-Exp1*, the RS codes are selected such that each RS-code block has seven bits. Four RS-codes output blocks are concatenated to form an input block of BCH codes.

During decoding, if the BCH code fails to correct the errors, it outputs a decoding failure flag. In such cases, the 28-bit output of the decoder, and therefore, all four RS-decoder input blocks, are treated as erasures. Assuming that there can be α errors and β erasures, the error correction capacity of RS codes is $2\alpha + \beta < d_{min}$, where d_{min} is the minimum distance of the RS-codes. Since we can predict the erasures for RS codes, they are operated in simultaneous error-erasure mode.

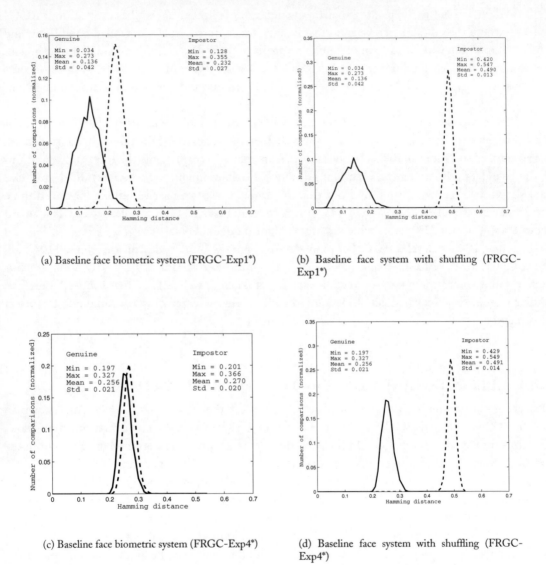

(a) Baseline face biometric system (FRGC-Exp1*)

(b) Baseline face system with shuffling (FRGC-Exp1*)

(c) Baseline face biometric system (FRGC-Exp4*)

(d) Baseline face system with shuffling (FRGC-Exp4*)

Figure 3.7: Normalized Hamming distance distributions for genuine and impostor comparisons on the NIST-FRGCv2 development data set for FRGC-Exp1* and FRGC-Exp4*. These are the same as shown in Fig. 2.9.

For the FRGC-Exp4*, we need 30% error correction. This is achieved by using Hadamard codes along with the zero insertion scheme. In this case, we used 7-bit RS blocks and Hadamard codes of size 64 bits. Fourteen zeros are uniformly inserted in every 50 bits of the face code thus forming 64-bit blocks. The Hadamard codes can correct 15 error bits in this block. Therefore, the effective error correction capacity is 15/50 = 0.3, because in each 64-bit block there are only 50 bits that can cause errors. The locations where the zeros are inserted are fixed and hence, the bits in those positions cannot cause errors.

3.5.3   EXPERIMENTAL RESULTS OF THE FACE-BASED KEY REGENERATION SYSTEM

The databases and associated experimental protocols for evaluating the proposed face-based system are already introduced in Section 3.5.1. We have carried out two separate experiments on face modality: FRGC-Exp1* (controlled vs controlled) and FRGC-Exp4* (controlled vs non-controlled). The results for these experiments on the development database are reported in Tables 3.8 and 3.9. Note that the amount of variations for FRGC-Exp1* is less as compared to that in FRGC-Exp4*. Hence, the zero insertion is not needed for FRGC-Exp1*. Because of the zero insertion and the different error correcting codes, the effective sizes of the face codes are different for the two experiments. Also, the zero insertion increases the face code length which enables to select higher length keys in case of FRGC-Exp4*. For these two experiments, the shuffling scheme is employed which increases the impostor Hamming distances such that there is no impostor comparison with Hamming distance less than the error correction capacity. For instance, in FRGC-Exp1* (on development data set), the minimum Hamming distance for impostor comparisons is 0.42 whereas the error correction capacity is 21.72%. Therefore, none of the key regeneration attempt for the impostor can be successful. This is reflected from the zero FAR in Table 3.8. Similar outcome can be observed for the FRGC-Exp4* where the minimum impostor Hamming distance is 0.429 whereas the error correction capacity is 30% resulting in zero FAR (Table 3.9).

As shown in Tables 3.8 and 3.10, the FRR for FRGC-Exp1 is not zero. As discussed earlier, increasing the error correction capacity is equivalent to increasing the verification threshold. Therefore, the FRR can be further decreased by increasing the error correction capacity. However, increasing the error correction capacity has one drawback. As shown in Section 2.4.2, if the shuffling key is compromised, the impostor Hamming distance overlaps with that of the baseline biometric system. It means that advantage gained from using the shuffling scheme is lost and the original Hamming distance distributions of the baseline biometric system come into effect. As can be seen in Fig. 3.7, the baseline system's Hamming distance curves for genuine and impostor comparisons have a large overlap which results in high recognition errors (FAR, FRR, EER, etc.). Therefore, if the shuffling key is compromised in a system having higher error correction capacity, the FAR will increase. Therefore, we decided not to increase the error correction capacity.

3.5.4   SECURITY ANALYSIS OF THE FACE-BASED KEY REGENERATION SYSTEM

Theoretical Security Analysis of the Face-Based Key Regeneration System
The crypto-bio keys obtained from the system described in this section are to be used for cryptographic purposes. It is required to estimate the theoretical entropy of such keys. The entropy analysis

Table 3.8: Results for the proposed system on NIST-FRGCv2 development data set, for FRGC-Exp1*; shuffling is applied on the face codes; $\approx$ 21.72% error correction; $n_s = 24$, $m = 7$; effective face code length=3,066; key length is in bits; FAR and FRR values are in %.

t_s	Key Length	FRGC-Exp1* Development	
		FAR	FRR
1	154	0	12.11
2	140	0	6.11
3	126	0	6.11
4	112	0	3.51
5	98	0	3.51
6	84	0	2.20
7	70	0	2.20
8	56	0	0.97

for the iris-based key regeneration system is already provided in Section 3.4.4. It is based on the estimation of the degrees of freedom in the biometric data and the error correction capacity of the ECC.

In case of face data, the two experiments (FRGC-Exp1* and FRGC-Exp4*) have different amounts of error correction, and hence, their entropy estimations must be carried out separately. There is no established method to calculate the degrees of freedom in face codes. However, such a method is proposed for iris by Daugman [47]. This method estimates the degrees of freedom from the impostor Hamming distance distribution since this distribution is Gaussian in nature. Since the impostor Hamming distance distribution in case of face modality is also Gaussian in nature, for the sake of completeness, the method used for iris described earlier in Section 3.4.4 is applied to face.

For the FRGC-Exp1*, the number of degrees of freedom calculated with Equation (3.8) in the un-shuffled face codes are $N = 227$ and that in the shuffled face codes are $N = 1,478$. The error correction capacity for FRGC-Exp1* is 21.72%. If the attacker attempts to guess the face code and password separately, the entropy contributed by the face codes is found to be 60-bits using Equation 3.7. The 52-bit password entropy is added to this resulting in the total entropy to be $60 + 52 = 112$ bits. If the attacker tries to guess the shuffled face data directly, the entropy is found to be 367 bits.

Similarly, for FRGC-Exp4*, there are $N = 447$ degrees of freedom in un-shuffled face codes while those in shuffled face codes are $N = 1,275$. When the attacker provides the face code and password separately, the entropy from face codes is 58-bit and adding the 52-bit entropy from

Table 3.9: Results for the proposed system on NIST-FRGCv2 development data set, for FRGC-Exp4*; shuffling is applied on the face codes and zeros are inserted; $\approx$ 30% error correction; $n_s = 64$, $m = 7$; effective face code length=4,096; key length is in bits; FAR and FRR values are in %.

t_s	Key Length	FRGC-Exp4* Development FAR	FRR
1	434	0	79.90
2	420	0	61.00
3	406	0	41.65
4	392	0	27.93
5	378	0	16.73
6	364	0	9.65
7	350	0	6.15
8	336	0	3.13
9	322	0	1.58
10	308	0	0.93
11	294	0	0.40
12	280	0	0.23
13	266	0	0
14	252	0	0
15	238	0	0
16	224	0	0

password, the total entropy becomes 110 bits. Providing the shuffled face codes directly result in 157-bit entropy.

The theoretically estimated entropies of the crypto-bio keys obtained with the iris- and face-based key regeneration systems are summarized in Table 3.12. It is interesting to see that the estimated entropy for face is higher than for iris. The important point highlighted by these results is that if the randomness in the biometric data is less, the increase in entropy because of the shuffling is higher. For example, as shown in Table 3.12, the entropy of the iris-based keys increases from 41 bits to 83 bits. But for face (FRGC-Exp1*), it increases from 60 bits to 367 bits.

Experimental Security Analysis of the Face-Based Key Regeneration System
As defined in the experimental methodology in Section 1.5.3, we carried out the security evaluation of the proposed face-based key regeneration system in two extreme scenarios: (a) stolen biometric scenario and (b) stolen key scenario.

Table 3.10: Results for the proposed system on NIST-FRGCv2 evaluation data set, for FRGC-Exp1*; shuffling is applied on the face codes; $\approx$ 21.72% error correction; $n_s = 24$, $m = 7$; effective face code length=3,066; key length is in bits; FAR and FRR values are in %.

t_s	Key Length	FRGC-Exp1* Evaluation FAR	FRR
1	154	0	11.05
2	140	0	5.60
3	126	0	5.60
4	112	0	2.63
5	98	0	2.63
6	84	0	1.14
7	70	0	1.14
8	56	0	0.63

In the stolen biometric scenario, an impostor always provides the stolen biometric data of a genuine user. But because of the involvement of the shuffling scheme, the false acceptance rate in this case still remains zero.

In the other security scenario, the stolen key scenario, an impostor always provides the correct shuffling key of the genuine user. In this case, the FAR increases than in the random impostor case. The values of FAR in these two security scenarios on the FRGC-Exp1* and FRGC-Exp4* experiments are reported in Table 3.13.

Note that, in both these cases, the FAR increases than the FAR for the random impostor case, in which the biometric as well as the key are assumed secret. We have seen that the shuffling scheme significantly improves the verification performance of the baseline biometric system. Therefore, if this shuffling scheme is not applied, then the FAR of the system increases. This FAR without shuffling is equal to the FAR of the proposed system in stolen key scenario. Thus, the use of shuffling prohibits an impostor who has stolen the biometric data while in the stolen key scenario, the system performs as good as the one without using shuffling.

3.6 EXTENSION OF THE PROPOSED KEY REGENERATION SCHEME TO OBTAIN CONSTANT LENGTH KEYS WITH HIGHER ENTROPY

The key regeneration scheme described in Section 3.3 can obtain keys from the biometric data. This system protects the biometric data by storing it in locked form. But, as reported in the results for this

Table 3.11: Results for the proposed system on NIST-FRGCv2 evaluation data set, Exp4 (FRGC-Exp4*); shuffling is applied on the face codes and zeros are inserted; $\approx$ 30% error correction; $n_s = 64, m = 7$; effective face code length=4,096; key length is in bits; FAR and FRR values are in %.

t_s	Key Length	FRGC-Exp4* Evaluation	
		FAR	FRR
1	434	0	77.18
2	420	0	55.10
3	406	0	38.40
4	392	0	24.07
5	378	0	15.47
6	364	0	9.35
7	350	0	5.52
8	336	0	3.20
9	322	0	1.55
10	308	0	0.93
11	294	0	0.65
12	280	0	0.25
13	266	0	0.15
14	252	0	0.05
15	238	0	0
16	224	0	0

scheme in Sections 3.4.3 and 3.5.3, the length of the key changes with the change in error correction capacity of the RS-codes[2]. However, cryptographic systems require cryptographic keys with fixed lengths (e.g., AES requires keys with 128, 192, or 256 bits). Therefore, in order to be compliant with such cryptosystems, the key regeneration scheme is extended in such a way that it can regenerate the reference biometric data protected in the system. This modified version of the scheme is shown in Fig. 3.8. The hash value of the reference biometric data can directly be used as a cryptographic key.

In this scheme, the regenerated key $\mathbf{K}'_r$ is re-encoded using the same error correction scheme as that used in the enrollment phase. When the errors between the enrollment and verification samples of the biometric data are within the error correction capacity of the ECC, the regenerated

---

[2]Strictly speaking, the hash value of the regenerated key can be used as a cryptographic key. It can be designed to have the same length irrespective of the length of the regenerated key.

Table 3.12: Theoretically estimated entropy for the proposed iris- and face-based key regeneration systems; Approach-1—The attacker provides the biometric data and password separately; Approach-2—The attacker directly provides the shuffled data.

Approach	Iris	Face: FRGC-Exp1	Face: FRGC-Exp4
Approach-1	93 (41+52)	112 (60+52)	110 (58+52)
Approach-2	83	367	157

Table 3.13: Experimental security analysis of the proposed face biometrics based crypto-bio key regeneration scheme in terms of FAR in %; FRGCv2 evaluation data set; stolen biometric—when face images of all the genuine users are stolen; stolen key—when the shuffling keys of all the users are stolen.

	FRGC-Exp1*			FRGC-Exp4*	
t_s	Stolen biometric	Stolen key	t_s	Stolen biometric	Stolen key
1	0	7.90	1	0	11.92
3	0	16.74	2	0	25.68
5	0	27.08	3	0	41.07
6	0	39.44	4	0	57.49

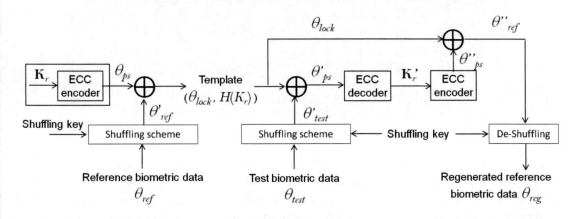

Figure 3.8: Extension of the key regeneration scheme proposed in Section 3.3 to obtain the enrollment biometric data. The hash value of this data will be used as a cryptographic key. This results in constant length keys and has higher entropy.

key $\mathbf{K}'_r$ is the same as the random key $\mathbf{K}_r$. Therefore, when the regenerated key $\mathbf{K}'_r$ is encoded with the ECC, the resultant encoded data θ''_{ps} is the same as the pseudo code θ_{ps}, because

$$\theta_{ps} = ECC(\mathbf{K}_r) \tag{3.9}$$

and

$$\mathbf{K}_r = \mathbf{K}'_r. \tag{3.10}$$

Therefore,

$$\theta''_{ps} = ECC(\mathbf{K}'_r) = ECC(\mathbf{K}_r) = \theta_{ps}. \tag{3.11}$$

The locked code θ_{lock} is obtained during the enrollment phase by XOR*ing* the modified biometric data (shuffled and in some cases zero padded) with the pseudo code θ_{ps}. Therefore, the modified biometric data can be regained from the locked code by XOR*ing* the θ''_{ps} with the locked code as:

$$\theta''_{ref} = \theta_{lock} \oplus \theta''_{ps} = \theta_{lock} \oplus \theta_{ps} = \theta'_{ref}. \tag{3.12}$$

If the scheme involves zero insertion, those zeros are present in θ''_{ref} and their locations are known. Therefore, these zeros can easily be removed. Since the reference biometric data is shuffled during enrollment, in order to obtain it back, de-shuffling is required. The schematic diagram of the de-shuffling process is shown in Fig. 3.9.

The de-shuffling process is exactly the reverse of the shuffling scheme. During shuffling, the shuffling key acts as a reference for moving the data blocks. In the same way, the de-shuffling key, denoted as $\mathbf{K}_{ds}$, functions as a reference for de-shuffling. In the shuffling process, the blocks, where the shuffling key-bit is one, are sorted out in the beginning and the remaining blocks are placed in the end in the shuffled data. Hence, in order to de-shuffle that data, the shuffled data is first divided into two parts, the contents of which are dependent on the de-shuffling key. We consider the length of the de-shuffling key (which is the same as that of the shuffling key) to be L_{sh} and each block of data is L_b-bits. The number of ones in the de-shuffling key are counted and that many blocks from the shuffled data are taken into Part-1, starting from the first. The remaining blocks are taken into Part-2.

An empty array $\mathbf{D}$ of size $L_{sh} \times L_b$ is initialized. The de-shuffling key is read bit-by-bit. If a bit at position i is one, a block from Part-1 is placed at the ith position in the array $\mathbf{D}$. If the bit is zero, a block from Part-2 is used instead. This process is carried out for all the bits in the de-shuffling key. At the end, the array $\mathbf{D}$ will contain blocks from the Part-1 and Part-2 distributed according to the de-shuffling key bit values. A pseudo code for the de-shuffling process is shown in Fig. 3.10.

As far as the shuffling and de-shuffling processes are concerned, if the de-shuffling key is the same as the shuffling key used during enrollment, the de-shuffled data is exactly same as the original data. Hence, considering the equation 3.12, and assuming the shuffling key provided is correct, the regenerated reference biometric data θ_{reg} is exactly same as the reference biometric data θ_{ref}. The hash value of this regenerated reference biometric data can be used as a cryptographic key. Irrespective of the error correction capacity t_s, the regenerated biometric data has a constant length.

This extended scheme completely relies on the fact that the regenerated key $\mathbf{K}'_r$ is same as the original random key $\mathbf{K}_r$. If these two keys are not the same, the system cannot recover the correct reference biometric data. Therefore, the result tables presented in Sections 3.4.3 and 3.5.3 also apply to this extended scheme.

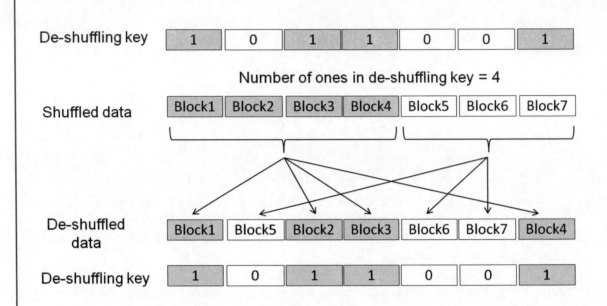

Figure 3.9: Schematic diagram of the de-shuffling process.

```
N = Total number of 1's in the de-shuffling_key;
Counter1 = 0;
Counter2 = 0;
for i = 1 to length of the de-shuffling_key,
    if de-shuffling_key(i) = 1,
        counter1 = counter1 + 1;
        deshuffled_data(i) = shuffled_data(counter1);
    else
        counter2 = counter2 + 1;
        deshuffled_data(i) = shuffled_data(N + counter2);
    end if
end for
```

Figure 3.10: Pseudo code for the de-shuffling algorithm.

The security analysis provided in Sections 3.4.4 and 3.5.4 can partially apply to this modified system. In that analysis, two approaches are reported which an attacker can chose: (a) to provide the biometric data and the shuffling key separately, and (b) by providing the shuffled data directly. The second approach (to provide the shuffled data directly) is not sufficient because even if the attacker regenerates the key $\mathbf{K}'_r$, he still needs to provide the de-shuffling key (which is same as the shuffling key) to regenerate the biometric data θ_{reg}. Therefore, an attacker must obtain the biometric data and the password separately in order to regenerate the key. Thus, the entropy of the keys in this scheme is equal to that obtained by the first approach. As shown in Table 3.12, the entropy is 93 bits in case of iris. Whereas the entropy in case of the FRGC-Exp1 experiment is 112 bits and in FRGC-Exp4, it is 110 bits.

3.7   CONCLUSIONS AND PERSPECTIVES

Obtaining high entropy keys using biometrics is a challenging problem. In this chapter, we propose a generalized scheme for biometrics-based cryptographic key regeneration. This scheme combines the ideas from cancelable biometrics and fuzzy commitment-based key regeneration. A shuffling-based cancelable transformation is applied on the biometric data and then this data is used in the fuzzy commitment-based scheme. The proposed key regeneration system is useful for generating high entropy keys strongly linked to the user's identity.

The generalized scheme is then adapted for two biometric modalities: iris and face. The most critical aspects of this adaptation are the selection of error correcting codes and tuning their error correction capacities according to the concerned biometric data.

Both the iris- and face-based key regeneration systems, satisfy the desired requirements of a crypto-biometric system: non-repudiation, revocability, template diversity, privacy protection, and high entropy keys. Since biometric data is required for regenerating the crypto-bio keys, it is difficult for someone to repudiate. The involvement of the shuffling scheme adds revocability, and template diversity to the system. The privacy of the user is protected in this system.

The estimated entropy of the crypto-bio keys obtained from iris is 83–93 bits. For the face-based system, the estimated entropy is 110–112 bits. The performance of the proposed systems is always better than the underlying baseline biometric system.

There are some issues that need to be solved regarding such key regeneration systems. For the intended operation of the proposed scheme, specific protocols need to be designed. The crypto-bio keys need to be shared between all the parties requiring secure communication link. In Chapter 4, we present some protocols which can share the crypto-bio keys obtained with the proposed schemes.

Another issue is the security analysis which should be extended to consider additional attacks. More importantly, an attacker may take advantage of different decoding mechanisms of the error correcting codes used in the system.

CHAPTER 4

Biometrics-Based Secure Authentication Protocols

4.1 INTRODUCTION

In previous chapters, we described two main types of crypto-biometric systems. The cancelable biometric systems proposed in Chapter 2 induce the important properties such as revocability, template diversity, and privacy protection into biometric systems. The biometrics-based key regeneration systems proposed in Chapter 3 can deliver long keys with high entropy. These crypto-bio keys, intended to be used in cryptographic applications, are obtained from biometrics and therefore are strongly linked to the user identity. The problem not addressed yet in these chapters, and largely ignored in most of the biometrics-based key (re)generation systems found in literature, is how to share these keys to be used in cryptography.

Cryptography is generally divided into two main categories: symmetric-key cryptography and public-key cryptography. Symmetric-key cryptography is better suited for real time data transfer because of its speed. In symmetric-key cryptography, the same key is used for encryption and decryption, and therefore it needs to be shared between all the parties. According to the Kerckhoffs' principle [88], the security of a cryptographic system lies in the key, and therefore, the cryptographic key needs to be protected. In order to share the key only with the intended users, different authentication mechanisms are employed.

In this chapter, we consider that there are two parties, a client and a server, who need to establish a secure communication link between them. As we defined in the glossary, authentication is a process in which one party (client or server) verifies the authenticity of the other, and then establishes a secure channel between them. In some systems, a process denoted as mutual authentication, is carried out in which both the parties authenticate each other. But, if a large amount of data encrypted with a single symmetric-key is available, several cryptanalytic attacks are made easier.

In public-key cryptography, the two parties, client and server, have their own pairs of public and private keys. The client encrypts a secret with the server's public key. This encrypted data can only be decrypted with the corresponding private key. Since only the server has access to this private key, only the server can perform the decryption and recover the secret. Therefore, technically speaking, public-key cryptography does not need to verify the authenticity of the other party. But, as described in Section 1.2.1 (page 6), the public-key cryptosystems are vulnerable to the man-in-the-middle attack [111]. An example of man-in-the-middle attack is shown in Fig. 1.4 (page 8). Therefore, the public-key cryptosystems also require authentication which is achieved by employing trusted third party certificates.

In order to overcome these shortcomings, many widely used cryptographic protocols, such as the Transport Layer Security (TLS) protocol [52][1], are hybrid systems that use public-key cryptography to exchange a symmetric key. This symmetric key is temporary, and is valid only for the current communication session. Such a symmetric key is denoted as session key. Having a temporary session key limits the amount of data encrypted with a single key. Moreover, the server authentication is carried out with the help of certificates issued by a certification authority trusted by both the parties. Additionally, the client can also be authenticated in a mutual authentication mode if he also obtains a certificate from the trusted certification authority.

The crypto-biometric systems summarized in Chapter 2 and 3 can be used for secure authentication in cryptographic communication. In fact, the crypto-bio key generation/regeneration systems do produce a key (as opposed to a single bit verification result of the biometric and cancelable biometric systems). This crypto-bio key can be used for secure cryptographic communication.

There are very few proposals found in literature for biometrics-based secure cryptographic protocols. A review of these systems is presented in Section 4.2. Most of those systems do not satisfy all the goals we set for crypto-biometric systems. Many of them require storage of biometric templates. Some others need a pre-existing secure channel for the biometric information exchange.

In this chapter, we present two protocols which enable us to share the crypto-bio keys securely. We make the following assumptions for these protocols.

- There is no trust between the client and the server. Therefore, the client will not pass the authenticators (e.g., biometric data, passwords, etc.) to the server. The server will also not share the stored information with the client.

- The communication link between the client and the server is unprotected. Therefore, the data being transferred through this link should not leak information.

- Biometric data of the user should not be stored in the server or database to protect the user's privacy. The stored data should be revocable.

- The protocol should achieve mutual authentication between the client and the server because none of them trust each other.

The first protocol is proposed in order to securely share the crypto-bio keys obtained with the key regeneration system described in Chapter 3. These keys are always the same for a particular user and can be used in symmetric cryptography. The second protocol is for generation and sharing of biometrics-based (crypto-bio) session keys. This protocol was first proposed in our recent work [81]. Both of these protocols achieve mutual authentication without the need of trusted third-party

---

[1]TLS is a widely used protocol, e.g., HTTPS (HyperText Transmission Protocol-Secure) uses TLS to secure World Wide Web traffic carried by HTTP. HTTPS is used for secure e-commerce applications such as online payments through the Internet, online banking applications, etc.

certificates. Since biometrics is involved in the crypto-bio key regeneration process, a strong link is established between the user's identity and his cryptographic keys. Additionally, the session key generation and sharing protocol allows easy online update of templates. This protocol can also be modified and extended in order to incorporate multiple biometric characteristics as we proposed in [83]. However, this modification is not covered in this chapter.

The rest of this chapter is organized as follows. In Section 4.2, a review of the crypto-biometrics-based key sharing protocols is presented. In Sections 4.3 and 4.4, the protocols for sharing crypto-bio keys and for generation and sharing of biometrics-based session keys, respectively, are described. Finally, conclusions and perspectives are given in Section 4.5.

4.2 BIOMETRICS-BASED SECURE CRYPTOGRAPHIC PROTOCOLS—STATE OF THE ART

The crypto-biometric systems described in the Sections 2.2 and 3.2 try to remove the limitations of the biometric and/or cryptographic systems. The cancelable biometric systems (Section 2.2.2) add revocability, template diversity, and privacy protection to the biometric systems. On the other hand, the systems described in Section 3.2, try to derive user-specific cryptographic keys, the authenticity of which is confirmed with the help of biometrics. A strong link is established between the user's identity and his cryptographic keys when the cryptographic keys are derived from biometrics. If properly designed, these systems can also have the important properties of revocability, template diversity, and privacy protection.

As mentioned in Chapter 1, cryptography is used to secure the information during storage and/or transmission. Cryptography is broadly divided into two types: symmetric-key cryptography in which the encryption and decryption keys are the same, and public-key (also called asymmetric) cryptography where the encryption and decryption keys are different but are mathematically related. In order to establish a cryptographically secure communication channel between all the entities participating in the information exchange, the correct cryptographic keys must be shared between them. Most of the crypto-biometric systems described in the previous section do not mention any specific key management/sharing methodologies. Those systems rely on conventional cryptography for the key sharing purpose and one side is still required to trust the other.

In this section, we present an overview of protocols that are specifically designed for sharing the crypto-bio keys or to create secure authenticated sessions based on biometrics. Note that we have not considered the protocols in which classical biometric comparison is used for authentication.

In 2005, Boyen et al. [26] proposed a biometrics based remote authentication protocol in which the fuzzy extractors [25] are used. The problem with this protocol is that it stores the reference biometric template along with the protected crypto-biometric template. Although this reference biometric template is not shared, it can still be considered as a privacy compromise.

The one-time biometric authentication protocol proposed by Ueshige and Sakurai [170] (2006) creates biometric authentication based secure sessions but it requires storage of classical biometric templates. In this protocol, a one-time transformation is generated which is unique to the session. This transformation is applied to the stored templates as well as the fresh biometric data. The comparison of the two transformed templates is carried out to establish the authenticity of the subject.

In 2007, Bringer et al. [29] employed the Goldwasser-Micali cryptosystem [63] for biometric authentication. This system allows the biometric comparison to be carried out in the encrypted domain. The proposed system requires storage of classical biometric templates. In order to protect the privacy, the system makes sure that the biometric data stored in the database cannot be explicitly linked to any user identity, but it only detects whether the data belonging to an identity is present in the database.

The "Secure Ad-hoc Pairing with Biometrics: SAfE" protocol proposed by Buhan et al. [31, 32] is a protocol which can be used to establish a secure link between two parties. Keys are obtained from biometrics with the help of the fuzzy extractor scheme. The drawback of this protocol is that it shares the biometric data between the two parties and requires mutual trust among them. Moreover, it also requires a secure channel for exchanging the biometric data.

Tang et al. [159] proposed an authentication protocol based on fuzzy extractor. This protocol provides security by employing the ElGamal public-key cryptosystem [55]. Cryptographic keys can be obtained and shared with this protocol while preserving some aspects of the user privacy. The drawback of this proposal is that it requires storage of biometric templates in a database. Additionally, it needs a secure communication link between the parties for exchanging the information.

In 2009, Fan et al. [57] proposed a three-factor remote authentication scheme using smart cards, passwords, and biometrics. In this scheme, they proposed to employ fuzzy sketch for securing a key and using the key regeneration on a smart card. Furthermore, the regenerated key is used for transformation of biometric data and public-key cryptography is used to share the transformed data with the server.

In 2009, Abid and Afifi [9] proposed a protocol for ePassport authentication based on elliptic curve cryptography. They proposed to employ biometrics, specifically fingerprints, to securely generate the parameters of the elliptic curve. These parameters are used for the ePassport bearer's authentication. This proposal is theoretical and no experimental evaluation is reported. The difficulty of this approach is that it requires a stable, constant input from biometrics which is practically not possible.

In [10], we integrated our work on iris based cryptographic key regeneration [77] with the Abid and Afifi scheme [9]. In this proposal, first a stable key is obtained from biometrics which is used to obtain the security parameters of the elliptic curve. This proposal can help integrate crypto-biometrics in ePassports.

Recently in 2010, Barni et al. [16] proposed a scheme for privacy preserving authentication based on fingerprints. This scheme employs the ElGamal cryptosystem which facilitates biometric comparison in encrypted domain. Upmanyu et al. [174, 175] proposed a blind authentication protocol which is also based on homomorphic encryption. Some other authentication protocols based on homomorphic encryption are [56, 103].

The drawback of the authentication protocols in [16, 29, 170, 175] is that they can only authenticate the subject. But they cannot produce the cryptographic keys required for secure communication. The protocols in [9, 26, 159] can share keys but these keys are the same for all the sessions. Using the same key for encryption of a large amount of data can make some cryptanalytic attacks easier. Therefore, most of the practical systems, e.g., the Transport Layer Security (TLS) protocol [52], employ a session specific symmetric key for secure communication. The session key is temporarily generated in every session. Public-key cryptographic protocols are used to share this key.

Following the same concept of session keys, in 2008–2009 Scheirer and Boult [149, 150] proposed "bipartite biotokens." They combined their earlier proposal of revocable biotokens [24] with fuzzy vaults [75] which enables to securely share keys using biometrics. In this scheme, a series of transformations is shared between the client and the server. A new transformation (in succession) is applied in every communication session. The bipartite biotokens are session specific and make it possible to share session specific data between two parties. The difference between our proposal and the scheme in [150] is in the key regeneration approach. The key regeneration system used in our protocol is a hybrid system combining a shuffling-based cancelable biometric system with fuzzy commitment scheme whereas [150] uses fuzzy vault scheme. Moreover, our scheme does not need any public key to initiate the key sharing process.

4.3   BIOMETRICS-BASED CRYPTOGRAPHIC KEY REGENERATION AND SHARING

In order to facilitate the understanding of the proposed protocols, the key regeneration system is revisited in the following subsection.

4.3.1   A RECAP OF THE BIOMETRICS-BASED KEY REGENERATION SCHEME

The biometrics-based key regeneration scheme shown in Fig. 4.1 is a hybrid system that combines a transformation based cancelable biometric system with fuzzy commitment-based key regeneration scheme. In this scheme, a key $\mathbf{K}_r$ is randomly generated and then encoded into a pseudo code θ_{ps} using Error Correcting Codes (ECC). A cancelable transformation is applied on the reference biometric data θ_{ref} of a user. This transformed data θ_{canc} is then XORed with the pseudo code θ_{ps} to obtain a locked code template θ_{lock}. At the time of key regeneration, a similar transformation is applied on the test biometric data θ_{test} and then the cancelable data θ'_{canc} is XORed with the stored template θ_{lock} to obtain θ'_{ps}. The two XOR operations transfer the errors between the reference and test biometric data onto the pseudo code ($\theta'_{ps} = \theta_{lock} \oplus \theta'_{canc} = \theta_{ps} \oplus \theta_{canc} \oplus \theta'_{canc} = \theta_{ps} \oplus e$). If the amount of errors e is less than the error correction capacity of the ECC, all these errors can be corrected after decoding. On successful error correction, a trial value of the random key $\mathbf{K}_r$, denoted as $\mathbf{K}'_r$ is obtained. A comparison of the hash values of these two keys is carried out, and if they are same, verification success is declared along with releasing the key. If the hash values are different, verification failure is declared.

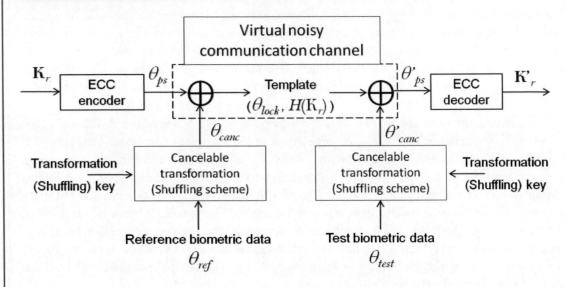

Figure 4.1: Biometrics-based key regeneration scheme described in Chapter 3.

The cancelable transformation used in our system is the shuffling scheme (Section 2.3). A randomly generated shuffling key K_{sh} is assigned to each user and this key is used to randomize the biometric data of that user. The biometric data is divided into blocks and these blocks are rearranged according to the shuffling key. Since the shuffling key is long, it needs to be stored on a smart card or should be generated using a password. The advantage of this shuffling scheme is that it increases only the impostor Hamming distances leaving the genuine Hamming distances intact. Hence, in addition to the properties of cancelability, revocability, template diversity, and privacy protection, the shuffling scheme also improves the verification performance of the system.

4.3.2   SECURE CRYPTO-BIO KEY SHARING PROTOCOL

Long keys having high entropy can be obtained with the key regeneration system proposed in Chapter 3 which is summarized in the previous subsection. Now, we propose a simple and effective protocol to securely share the crypto-biometric keys obtained with this system.

A schematic diagram of the proposed protocol for crypto-biometric key sharing is shown in Fig. 4.2. The enrollment process (not shown in the figure) is carried out off-line at a secure location. It is basically the same as described in Section 4.3.1. A secure, locked code template θ_{lock} is created using a random key K_r, shuffling key K_{sh}, and the reference biometric data θ_{ref}. This θ_{lock} along with the hash of the key K_r, i.e., $H(K_r)$ is stored in a database. The system can also employ a smart card to store the shuffling key K_{sh} in encrypted form. Otherwise, the shuffling key can be directly generated from a password.

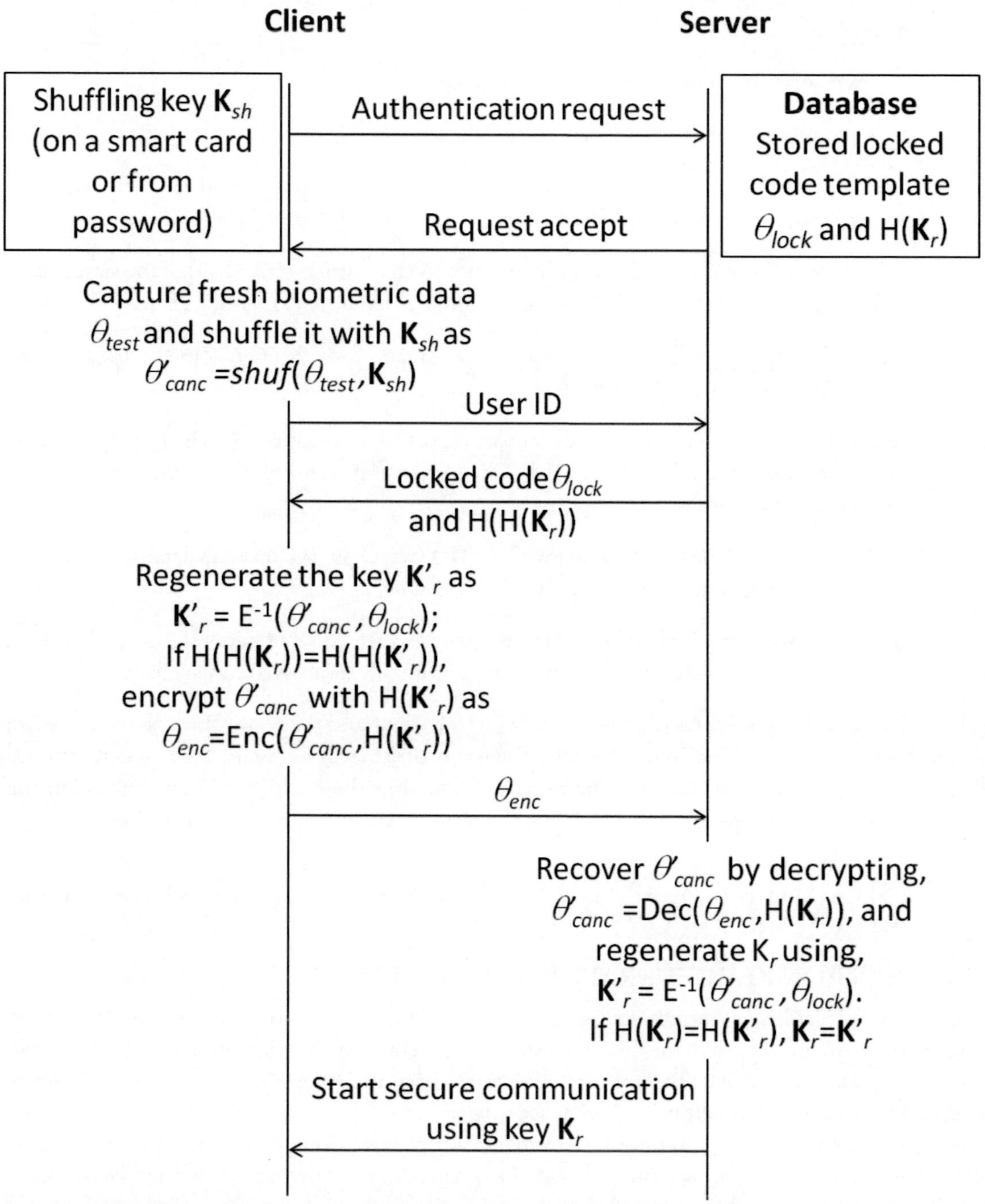

Client   **Server**

Shuffling key K_{sh} (on a smart card or from password)		**Database** Stored locked code template θ_{lock} and $H(K_r)$

Authentication request →

Request accept ←

Capture fresh biometric data θ_{test} and shuffle it with K_{sh} as $\theta'_{canc} = shuf(\theta_{test}, K_{sh})$

User ID →

Locked code θ_{lock} and $H(H(K_r))$ ←

Regenerate the key K'_r as $K'_r = E^{-1}(\theta'_{canc}, \theta_{lock})$; If $H(H(K_r)) = H(H(K'_r))$, encrypt θ'_{canc} with $H(K'_r)$ as $\theta_{enc} = Enc(\theta'_{canc}, H(K'_r))$

θ_{enc} →

Recover θ'_{canc} by decrypting, $\theta'_{canc} = Dec(\theta_{enc}, H(K_r))$, and regenerate K_r using, $K'_r = E^{-1}(\theta'_{canc}, \theta_{lock})$. If $H(K_r) = H(K'_r)$, $K_r = K'_r$

Start secure communication using key K_r ←

Figure 4.2: The proposed protocol for biometrics-based secure key sharing.

At a later time, when the client needs a secure cryptographic key for communication, the following steps are carried out.

1. The client sends the authentication request to the server.

2. The server responds with the request accept signal.

3. At the client side, fresh biometric data θ_{test} of the user is captured and shuffled using the shuffling key $\mathbf{K}_{sh}$ to obtain shuffled test code θ'_{canc}. Only the user ID is sent to the server.

4. The server sends the locked code θ_{lock} along with the hash value $H(H(\mathbf{K}_r))$ of the stored hash (i.e., hash of $H(\mathbf{K}_r)$) of the user corresponding to the requested ID to the client.

5. At the client side, a key $\mathbf{K}'_r$ is obtained from θ_{lock} and θ'_{canc} as, $\mathbf{K}'_r = E^{-1}(\theta'_{canc}, \theta_{lock})$ where $E^{-1}(\cdot)$ indicates the decoding function.

6. The client computes $H(H(\mathbf{K}'_r))$ and compares it with the received $H(H(\mathbf{K}_r))$ and if the two values are equal, the shuffled biometric data θ'_{canc} is encrypted using $H(\mathbf{K}'_r)$ and the encrypted data is sent to the server.

7. The server decrypts the received data with $H(\mathbf{K}_r)$ (which is stored in the database) to obtain θ'_{canc} and then regenerates the key $\mathbf{K}'_r$ from θ_{lock} and θ'_{canc}.

8. The server checks the hash values of the original and regenerated keys ($H(\mathbf{K}_r)$ and $H(\mathbf{K}'_r)$, respectively). If they are equal, it sends a start communication signal to the client.

Thus, a secure channel is established between the client and the server through which secure communication can be carried out. Moreover, the protocol achieves biometric based secure authentication over an unsecured channel. The templates stored in the database are cancelable and the system possesses the properties of revocability, template diversity, and privacy protection.

4.4 BIOMETRICS-BASED SESSION-KEY GENERATION AND SHARING PROTOCOL

4.4.1 SESSION KEY GENERATION AND SHARING

The protocol described in the previous section is for sharing crypto-bio keys which can be used in symmetric cryptographic systems. Having a single symmetric key for encrypting a large amount of data is not good for security. Therefore, it is essential to have a scheme which can generate and share session keys based on biometrics for higher security.

In this section, we propose a novel protocol to generate and share session keys based on biometrics. It makes use of the biometrics based key regeneration system described in Section 4.3.1, but it can be generalized to accommodate any other key regeneration scheme. The enrollment is securely carried out off-line during which a cancelable template is generated from the enrollment biometric data of the user and is stored in the database at the server. In our case, the cancelable template is the shuffled biometric data θ_{canc} which is obtained by shuffling the enrollment biometric data θ_{ref} with a shuffling key $\mathbf{K}_{sh}$. The shuffling key $\mathbf{K}_{sh}$ is either stored on a smart card or can be generated from a password.

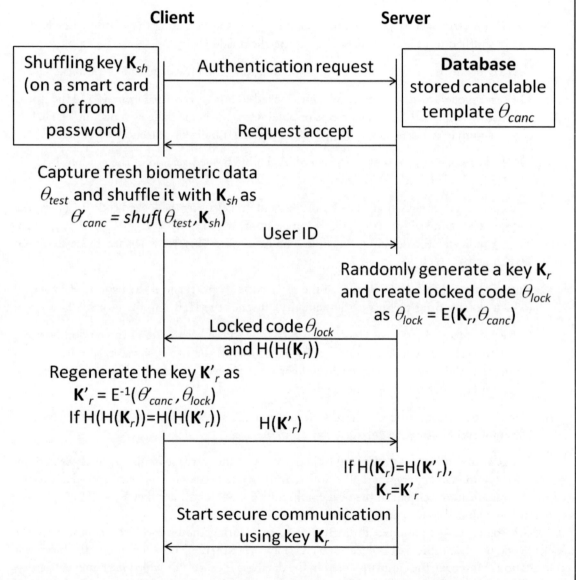

Figure 4.3: The proposed protocol for generating and sharing biometrics-based session keys.

Figure 4.3 shows a schematic diagram of the proposed session key generation and sharing protocol. The channel between the client and the server is not secure, and hence, no private or sensitive information should be sent over the network unless the channel is secured. When a client desires to securely communicate with the server, the following steps are carried out.

1. The client sends authentication request to the server.

2. The server sends acknowledgement to the client.

3. Fresh biometric data θ_{test} of the user is captured and shuffled using the shuffling key $\mathbf{K}_{sh}$ to obtain shuffled test biometric data θ'_{canc} at the client side.

4. User ID of the user is sent to the server. Note that the biometric data is not sent to the server.

5. The server generates a random key $\mathbf{K}_r$ and a locked code θ_{lock} is created from $\mathbf{K}_r$ and the stored cancelable template θ_{canc}. This process of obtaining θ_{lock} is the same as shown in Fig. 4.1. It can be summarized as $\theta_{lock} = E(\mathbf{K}_r, \theta_{canc})$ where $E(\cdot)$ indicates the encoding function.

6. The locked code θ_{lock} is sent to the client. A double hashed version of the random key, i.e., $H(H(\mathbf{K}_r))$ is also sent to the client.

7. The client regenerates a trial value $\mathbf{K}'_r$ of the random key using the locked code θ_{lock}, and the shuffled test biometric data θ'_{canc}. This can be summarized as $\mathbf{K}'_r = E^{-1}(\theta'_{canc}, \theta_{lock})$, where $E^{-1}(\cdot)$ indicates the decoding function. The regenerated key $\mathbf{K}'_r$ is hashed twice to obtain $H(\mathbf{K}'_r)$ and $H(H(\mathbf{K}'_r))$.

8. The client compares $H(H(\mathbf{K}'_r))$ with the received $H(H(\mathbf{K}_r))$ and if the two values are equal (which also confirms the server's authenticity), it sends the $H(\mathbf{K}'_r)$ to the server.

9. Server compares the received hash value $H(\mathbf{K}'_r)$ with the hash value of the random key $\mathbf{K}_r$, i.e., with $H(\mathbf{K}_r)$ to check the authenticity of the user. If the two hash values are the same, it means that the user is authentic and has correctly received the randomly generated key $\mathbf{K}_r$. Thus, both parties have the same key $\mathbf{K}_r$.

10. The key $\mathbf{K}_r$ is then treated as a session key and the server sends the signal to start secure communication using the key $\mathbf{K}_r$.

Thus, at the end of this protocol, the client as well as the server share the same key which can be used for symmetric-key cryptography. Note that the key is temporary and is destroyed at the end of the communication session. In the next communication session, a new key $\mathbf{K}_r$ will be randomly generated and shared to be used as a session key.

The data being transferred through the channel during the protocol are request, user ID, locked code θ_{lock}, and the hash values $H(H(\mathbf{K}_r))$ and $H(\mathbf{K}'_r)$, none of which reveal the biometric information. Moreover, the template stored in the database is cancelable which itself prevents cross-linking between biometric databases and protects user privacy.

As opposed to the popular and widely used cryptographic protocols such as TLS, the proposed protocol does not need a third-party trusted certification authority. In TLS, the third-party certification is used to confirm the server authenticity by using digital certificates. In our proposed protocol, client can confirm the authenticity of the server by comparing the double hashed values $H(H(\mathbf{K}'_r))$ and $H(H(\mathbf{K}_r))$. This comparison can yield positive result only if the server has generated a locked code θ_{lock} from the stored template θ_{canc} of the same user. On the other hand, the server authenticates the client by comparing the hash values $H(\mathbf{K}_r)$ and $H(\mathbf{K}'_r)$. Thus, our protocol achieves mutual authentication without the need of third-party certificates. The system described here employs strong authentication by combining biometrics with password (or smart card). Since the user is required to provide specific information in addition to biometric data, the system can resist replay attacks.

The error correction coding is applied at the time of authentication/key regeneration. Hence, it is possible to accommodate different error correcting codes (compatible with the biometric data) in the protocol. As it is done in the TLS, the client and server can negotiate on the choice of ECC and the error correction capacity to be used during authentication.

4.4.2   ONLINE TEMPLATE UPDATE

Many systems (such as online banking services) require that the user authentication credentials be updated periodically. In password-based systems, this means that the user is asked to change his password periodically. On the other hand, the user may also wish to change his credentials.

The distributed nature of our proposed protocol allows the user and/or the system to update the template online. The template update procedure involves changing the cancelable template θ_{canc} by changing the reference biometric data θ_{ref} and the shuffling key $\mathbf{K}_{sh}$. The procedure for this template update is shown in Fig. 4.4.

The steps followed during the template update procedure are as follows.

1. A secure communication channel is created between the client and the server by using the session key generation and sharing protocol described in the previous subsection (shown in Fig. 4.3).

2. A new shuffling key $\mathbf{K}'_{sh}$ is randomly generated at the client side and a cancelable template θ'_{canc} is obtained from the fresh test biometric data θ_{test} and $\mathbf{K}'_{sh}$.

3. The new cancelable template θ'_{canc} is sent to the server through the encrypted channel.

4. The server compares the old template stored in the database θ_{canc} with the received cancelable template θ'_{canc}. If the Hamming distance between the two is less than a threshold, the old template θ_{canc} is replaced with the new one θ'_{canc}. Update success/failure message is sent to the client.

5. If the received message is success, the old shuffling key $\mathbf{K}_{sh}$ stored on the smart card is replaced with the new one $\mathbf{K}'_{sh}$.

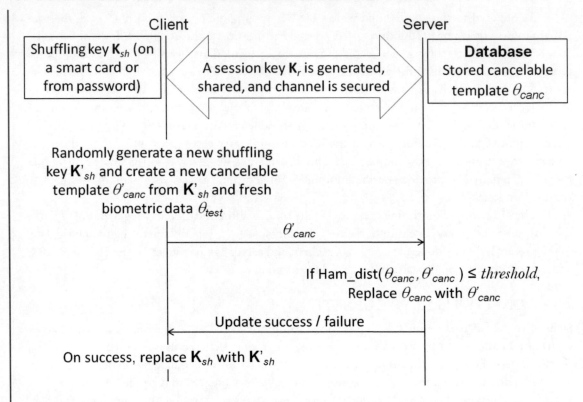

Figure 4.4: Protocol showing online template update. In the beginning of this protocol, the mutual authentication between the client and the server is carried out with the protocol shown in Fig. 4.3. Ham_dist means Hamming distance.

Note that the template update process can be initialized by either the client or the server. Also, the mutual authentication between client and server is carried out before initiating the template update procedure during session key generation and sharing. We recommend that template update should be carried after every session for higher security.

The proposed protocol can also be integrated inside classical cryptographic protocols such as TLS. Such classical protocols can first be used to establish a secure connection between the client and the server. Then the protocol shown in Fig. 4.3 can be employed for biometrics-based secure mutual authentication between the client and the server.

4.5 CONCLUSIONS AND PERSPECTIVES

In this chapter, the important issue of application of the crypto-bio keys obtained from the biometrics-based key regeneration systems is addressed. To begin with, we proposed a novel protocol which enables sharing of the crypto-bio keys between two parties (a client and a server) over a completely un-secure communication channel. The limitation of this protocol is that the crypto-bio keys obtained during its execution are always the same. In order to have better security, we proposed a new protocol which enables generation and sharing of biometrics based session keys. The session keys are precisely valid for a single communication session and are destroyed afterwards. Both of these two protocols achieve mutual authentication between the client and the server in a zero trust environment (client does not trust the server and vice-versa). The underlying key regeneration scheme, and in turn, these protocols, possess the properties of revocability, template diversity, and privacy protection.

CHAPTER 5

Concluding Remarks

5.1 SUMMARY

Biometrics and cryptography are two techniques which have high potential for providing information security. Unfortunately, both of these have certain limitations. Cryptography requires keys, but these keys are not strongly bound to the user's identity, whereas, biometrics suffer from nonrevocability, lack of template diversity, and possibility of privacy compromise. A combination of biometrics and cryptography is a good solution for eliminating these limitations. Such systems, in which biometrics and cryptography are combined, are denoted as crypto-biometric systems in this text.

This is an emerging field which started from the late 1990's, and lacks a uniform terminology. Therefore, first of all, a systematic classification of the crypto-biometric systems found in literature is presented based on their principal goals and working methodologies. We proposed two major classes: (i) protection of biometric data and (ii) obtaining biometrics-based cryptographic keys. The systems in these two categories were further classified based on their working methodology. This classification can help other researchers to position their systems related to the state of the art.

A cancelable biometric system is described in Chapter 2 to protect the biometric data. A user-specific shuffling technique was proposed which adds revocability and template diversity to the biometric systems. Additionally, it protects the biometric data privacy, information privacy, and identity privacy of the user. The most important advantage of this shuffling technique is that it improves the verification performance of the baseline biometric system by more than 80%. The reason for this improvement is that the shuffling scheme increases the impostor Hamming distances without changing the genuine Hamming distances. A distinctive feature of this scheme is that, if the shuffling key for all the users is compromised, its performance is equal to that of the baseline biometric system. This is a distinct advantage of this system with respect to other systems found in literature.

It is a well-known fact among the biometrics research community that the biometric data coming from a single source contain variability. In classical biometric systems, a similarity score between the query and the target sample is calculated first. This score is compared with a threshold in order to take the verification success/failure decision. However, in biometrics-based cryptographic key regeneration systems, the goal is to output a multi-bit string depending on the biometric data. This is achieved by employing Error Correcting Codes (ECC) in a fuzzy commitment scheme where biometric data matching is transformed into an error correction problem. In Chapter 3, a key regeneration type crypto-biometric system is presented. In this system, the shuffling scheme is combined with a fuzzy commitment-based system to develop a hybrid scheme for biometrics-based cryptographic key regeneration. This hybrid system illustrates how two basic crypto-biometric systems (a transformation based cancelable biometric system and a fuzzy commitment-based key regeneration scheme) can be combined in order to have a more secure system with the desired characteristics.

The shuffling scheme is applied on the biometric features to make them cancelable. The cancelable features are then used in a fuzzy commitment-based key regeneration system. This scheme possesses the important properties of revocability and template diversity, and it also protects user's privacy. This generic scheme was adapted for iris and face modalities. The estimated entropy of the crypto-bio keys obtained from iris is 83–93 bits. For the face-based system, the estimated entropy is 110–112 bits.

Finally, the important problem of securely sharing the crypto-bio keys is addressed in Chapter 4. Crypto-biometric key sharing is largely overlooked in many crypto-biometric system designs. In fact, sharing the crypto-biometric keys is as important as generating them. These protocols can share the crypto-bio keys while achieving mutual authentication between a client and a server. The protocol also allows sharing of session specific (one-time) crypto-bio keys with the help of biometrics. This protocol operates in a zero trust environment and achieves mutual authentication without the need of trusted third party certificates. Session keys have high practical importance, and therefore, the biometrics-based session key generation and sharing protocol can find a large number of applications. This protocol has a potential to replace the existing key sharing protocols. On the other hand, it can be seamlessly integrated into classical key sharing protocols to provide additional level of security.

5.2 FUTURE RESEARCH DIRECTIONS

The crypto-biometric systems described in this text can be further adapted to different biometric modalities. Open source biometric reference systems, such as the BioSecure reference systems available at [2], can be very useful for this purpose. Moreover, the systems can further be tested on larger databases.

The crypto-biometric systems as well as the biometrics-based session key generation and sharing protocol can further be extended to integrate multi-biometrics. Using multi-biometrics has many advantages over uni-biometrics such as better verification accuracy, larger feature space to accommodate more subjects, and higher security against spoofing. Additionally, it can provide longer keys having higher entropy.

It has been observed that the noninvertibility and performance improvement properties of the cancelable biometric systems are contradictory to each other. Indeed, if a cancelable transformation is noninvertible, it generally degrades the verification performance. The transformations that improve the verification performance are generally invertible. A problem for future research could be to design a noninvertible cancelable transformation which improves verification performance.

APPENDIX A

Baseline Biometric Systems, Databases, and Experimental Protocols

A.1 BASELINE SYSTEMS USED FOR EXTRACTING FEATURES FROM BIOMETRIC DATA

A.1.1 BASELINE OPEN SOURCE IRIS SYSTEM—OSIRISV1

The Open Source Iris Recognition System—OSIRISv1, developed under the BioSecure framework [3], described in [93] (available online at [1])—is used for extracting binary iris code features from iris images. The circular iris region first needs to be detected correctly using a process called iris segmentation. In order that our system is not influenced by segmentation errors, we manually adjusted the segmentation if necessary. The segmented circular iris region is then converted into a rectangular image of fixed size using Daugman's rubber sheet model [48]. In our experiments, the size of the normalized images is 512×80 pixels. The normalized image is decomposed using Gabor filters and phase information from the decomposed images is binarized and concatenated to form a one-dimensional binary iris code. In all our experiments, the extracted iris codes are 1,188 bits long. Figure A.1 shows an iris image at different processing levels.

The iris codes obtained from the reference and test iris images are compared using the Hamming distance. Generally, in such systems, noise masks are employed to eliminate noisy portions of the iris image from comparison. Equation (A.1) gives the formula for calculating the Hamming distance:

$$\text{Hamming distance} = \frac{\|(codeA \oplus codeB) \cap maskA \cap maskB\|}{\|maskA \cap maskB\|}. \tag{A.1}$$

In this equation, $codeA$ and $codeB$ are the iris codes from imageA and imageB whereas maskA and maskB are their respective noise masks. From this equation, it is clear that the reference noise mask is required to be logically AND*ed* with the test mask for Hamming distance calculation and therefore, needs to be stored. In our crypto-biometric systems, this may leak information about the reference biometric template. Therefore, we do not take the noise masks into consideration. This makes the crypto-biometric system design more challenging. Instead, we use a static mask which

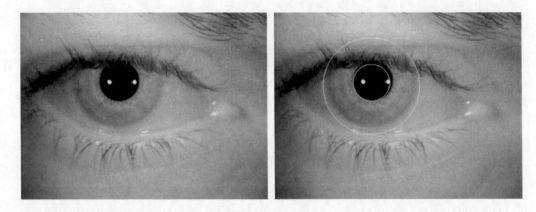

(a) Raw iris image (from CBS database)   (b) Segmented image showing the location of the iris

(c) Normalized iris image

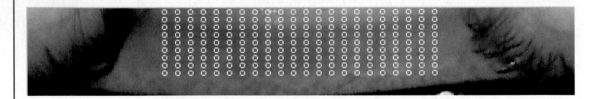

(d) Normalized iris image showing the locations at which the binary features are calculated

Figure A.1: Illustration of processing of an iris image: (a) raw iris image; (b) segmented iris image; (c) normalized iris image; and (d) normalized iris image with the locations where Gabor filters are applied for binary feature extraction.

eliminates the probable noisy regions such as the possible locations of eyelids and eyelashes. An example of a normalized image along with the fixed mask is shown in Fig. A.1(d).

During acquisition, there is a possibility of rotation of iris due to head tilt. In order to cope with such iris rotations, the OSIRISv1 shifts the normalized test iris image horizontally in both directions. The iris codes extracted from such rotated images are compared with the reference iris code using the Hamming distance metric and the minimum of these Hamming distances is considered for comparison with a threshold. In OSIRISv1, the normalized test iris image is shifted 10 times in both directions thus resulting in 21 comparisons. For our crypto-biometric systems, we need only the binary feature vectors from OSIRISv1. Therefore, the rotation adjustment module is re-implemented and validated experimentally.

A.1.2   BASELINE FACE SYSTEM

The key regeneration systems described in this text are based on the fuzzy commitment scheme [76]. It requires that the biometric data are represented as an ordered set of binary values. In order to extract a binary face code from the face images, first a Gabor filter-based approach is employed [95]. The face image is geometrically normalized using program from the CSU Face Recognition Evaluation System [20], and then processed using log-Gabor filters having four scales and eight orientations using the MATLAB source code available at [92]. Magnitude of the filtered output is calculated, downsampled, and concatenated to form a 3,200-element feature vector. The values of this vector are then binarized to obtain a 3,200-bit string called face code. The binarization process used is very simple. The median of the values of each feature vector is taken as a threshold. The elements having higher value than the threshold are converted to one while the remaining are converted to zeros.

The reason for using such a basic approach for a baseline face recognition system is that, in order to obtain long keys with the fuzzy commitment scheme, the length of the feature vector should be high. There are many other baseline face systems such as the SudParis Face Recognition system (SudFROG) [132] which perform better than the one used in this text. But, in SudFROG, after applying the Gabor filters to the normalized face images, dimensionality reduction technique called DLDA are used. This results in the feature vector with very small size. Therefore, it cannot be used for our key regeneration systems in its present status.

Some other possible binarization mechanisms (which are applied to fingerprints) are summarized in [169]. These techniques are: simple binarization, reliable component selection [85, 89], and Detection Rate Optimized Bit Allocation (DROBA) [41]. These binarization mechanisms take multiple samples as input and use statistical characteristics such as mean and standard deviation of the genuine distribution for determining the quantization threshold. Using these binarization methods can improve the verification performance of the system. However, these methods require storage of user-specific auxiliary information needed for the binarization step during verification. This auxiliary information is highly sensitive and may leak information about the biometric data and user identity. Indeed, the stored auxiliary information from different systems can be used for cross-matching between databases thus compromising privacy, one of the main goals of the proposed systems.

When compared to these approaches, the binarization method used in our system has an advantage that it does not require storage of any user-specific information for binarization. In this way, the problem of information leakage is eliminated. Moreover, the median of the feature vector is used as binarization threshold. This ensures that there are nearly equal number of zeros and ones in the binary feature vector.

A.2   DATABASES AND EXPERIMENTAL PROTOCOLS

Evaluation of the systems described in this book is carried out by testing the system on publicly available databases. Moreover, the development data set is different than the test data set without overlap. Various parameters of the crypto-biometric systems, such as, length of the shuffling key, choice of ECC and error correction capacity, are tuned on the development database. The systems are later tested on the evaluation data sets using these parameters. The databases used for iris as well as face, along with their associated experimental protocols, are described in the following subsections.

A.2.1   IRIS DATABASES AND EXPERIMENTAL PROTOCOLS

For iris, two databases are used namely Casia-BioSecure (CBS) database [93] (OKI device subset) for development and NIST-ICE database [131] for performance evaluation.

The CBS database is composed of two parts: CBS-BiosecureV1 and CBS-CasiaV2. Each of these two parts contains 1,200 images from 60 eyes of 30 persons with 20 images from each eye. According to the protocol described in [93], each of these data sets is divided into two parts as:

1. enrollment data set consisting of the first 10 images of each eye; and

2. test data set composed of the remaining 10 images.

For intra-class comparisons, the 10 images from enrollment data set are compared to the 10 images of the same eye from the test data set. For inter-class comparisons, the enrollment data set images are compared with 10 randomly selected images from other eyes from the test data set. This results in comparisons between images obtained in different sessions and different illumination conditions, and between images of eyes with and without glasses. In total, there are 6,000 genuine and 6,000 impostor comparisons for the two data sets—CBS-BiosecureV1 and CBS-CasiaV2.

Once the system parameters are tuned on the CBS database, the system is evaluated on the NIST-ICE database [131]. This database consists of 2,953 images obtained from 244 eyes of 132 users. 124 users have recorded right eye images while 120 have recorded left eye images with 112 users being present in both these sets. As described in the ICE protocol [131], two different experiments are carried out for this database. Experiment-1 (ICE-exp1) consists of comparison of right eye images while Experiment-2 (ICE-Exp2) consists of left eye comparisons. All possible comparisons between image pairs are carried out for each of these experiments. In total, 12,214 genuine and 1,002,386 impostor comparisons were carried out in ICE-Exp1, whereas in ICE-exp2, 14,653 genuine, and 1,151,975 impostor comparisons were performed.

A.2.2   FACE DATABASE AND EXPERIMENTAL PROTOCOLS

For our experiments on face modality, a subset of the FRGCv2 (Face Recognition Grand Challenge version 2) face database [130, 133] is selected. The full FRGCv2 database contains images from 466 subjects and is composed of 16,028 controlled still images captured under controlled conditions and 8,024 non-controlled still images captured under uncontrolled lighting conditions. There are two types of expressions: smiling and neutral and a large time variability exists. There are many experiments defined in order to evaluate the performance of algorithms for different sets of parameters.

The crypto-biometric systems described in this book have much more computational complexity than the baseline biometric systems. Therefore, a significantly more amount of time is required to carry out the performance evaluation. Moreover, there are multiple test that need to be carried out for different parameters of the crypto-biometric systems. This poses practical difficulties for running the full experimental protocols defined for the FRGCv2 database. In order to reduce the number of comparisons, we selected a subset of the FRGCv2 database for our experiments.

Our data set consists of 250 subjects each of which has 12 facial images. Out of these 250 users, the first 125 users are used for development and the remaining 125 are used for evaluation purposes, thus there is no overlap between the development and evaluation data sets. The images in FRGCv2 database are captured under two different acquisition conditions: controlled and uncontrolled. The controlled images taken in a studio setting are full-frontal facial images taken under two lighting conditions and with two facial expressions (smiling and neutral). The uncontrolled images were taken in varying illumination conditions, e.g., hallways, atriums, or outside. Each set of uncontrolled images contains two expressions, smiling and neutral. Examples of face images from controlled and uncontrolled sets are shown in Fig. A.2. Among the 12 images of a person, the first are from the controlled set and remaining four are from the uncontrolled set. Two separate experiments are carried out: FRGC-exp1*—in which, the images from the controlled set are taken for enrollment as well as test; and FRGC-exp4*—where the enrollment images are taken from the controlled set and those from uncontrolled set are used as tests (query). We put the star (*) in order to stress the fact that these experiments are not exactly the same as described in the full FRGCv2 protocols. For the FRGC-exp1*, 3,500 genuine and 496,000 impostor comparisons are carried out while for FRGC-exp4*, 4,000 genuine and 496,000 impostor comparisons are done.

(a) An example image from the controlled set   (b) An example image from the non-controlled set

Figure A.2: Examples of images from the FRGCv2 database: (a) an image from the controlled set; and (b) an image from the non-controlled set of the same subject.

APPENDIX B

BioSecure Tool for Performance Evaluation

The performance of the biometric systems (in terms of FAR, FRR, and EER) along with their error margins for 90% confidence intervals is calculated with the help of the BioSecure performance evaluation tool [132]. The method for estimating the confidence intervals in this tool is described below.

B.1 PARAMETRIC CONFIDENCE INTERVAL ESTIMATION

It is clear that in a biometric system performance evaluation experiment it is not possible to cover the whole human population. The score distribution that we obtain is a subset of the complete population. Therefore, the verification error rates (e.g., EER, OP) obtained during the evaluation can be erroneous. In order to predict the possible error margins, a 90% interval of confidence is calculated. The method described here is the one proposed by Bolle et al. [22].

Suppose we have M client scores and N impostor scores. We denote these sets of scores by $\mathbf{X} = \{X_1, ..., X_M\}$ and $\mathbf{Y} = \{Y_1, ..., Y_N\}$, respectively. In the following, we assume that available scores are similarity measures.

Let $\mathbf{S}$ be the set of thresholds used to calculate the score distributions.

For the set of client scores, $\mathbf{X}$, assume that this is a sample of M numbers drawn from a population with distribution F, that is, $F(x) = Prob(X \leq x), x \in \mathbf{S}$.

Let the impostor scores $\mathbf{Y}$ be a sample of N numbers drawn from a population with distribution $G(y) = Prob(Y \leq y), y \in S$.

In this way, $FRR(x) = F(x)$ and $FAR(y) = 1 - G(y), x$ and $y \in \mathbf{S}$. From now on, we have to find an estimate of these distributions at some threshold $t_0 \in \mathbf{S}$ and then, we have to estimate the confidence interval for these estimations.

- The estimate of $F(t_0)$ using data $\mathbf{X}$ is the unbiased statistic:

$$\hat{F}(t_0) = \frac{1}{M} \sum_{i=1}^{M} 1(X_i \leq t_0). \tag{B.1}$$

Thus, $\hat{F}(t_0)$ is obtained by simply counting the $X_i \in \mathbf{X}$ that are smaller than t_0 and dividing by M.

In the same way, the estimate $G(t_0)$ using the data $\mathbf{Y}$ is the unbiased statistic:

$$\hat{G}(t_0) = \frac{1}{N} \sum_{i=1}^{N} 1(Y_i \leq t_0). \tag{B.2}$$

- In the following, let us concentrate on the distribution F. For the moment, let us keep $x = t_0$ and let us determine the confidence interval for $\hat{F}(t_0)$.

First define Z as a binomial random variable, the number of successes, where success means $(X \leq t_0)$ is true, in M trials with probability of success $F(t_0) = Prob(X \leq t_0)$. This random variable Z has binomial probability mass distribution:

$$P(Z = z) = \binom{M}{z} F(t_0)^z (1 - F(t_0))^{M-z}, \quad z = 0, ..., M. \tag{B.3}$$

The expectation of Z is $E(Z) = MF(t_0)$ and the variance is $\sigma^2(Z) = MF(t_0)(1 - F(t_0))$.

From this, it follows that the random variable Z/M has expectation $F(t_0)$ and variance $F(t_0)(1 - F(t_0))/M$. When M is large enough, using the law of large numbers, Z/M is distributed according to a normal distribution, i.e., $Z/M \sim \mathcal{N}(F(t_0), F(t_0)(1 - F(t_0))/M)$.

Now it can be seen that, $\hat{Z}/M = \hat{F}(t_0)$. Hence, for large M, $\hat{F}(t_0)$ is normally distributed with an estimate of the standard deviation given by:

$$\hat{\sigma}(t_0) = \sqrt{\frac{(\hat{F}(t_0))(1 - \hat{F}(t_0))}{M}}. \tag{B.4}$$

The confidence intervals can be determined from $\hat{\sigma}(t_0)$. For example, a 90% interval of confidence is:

$$F(t_0) \in [\hat{F}(t_0) - 1.645\hat{\sigma}(t_0), \hat{F}(t_0) + 1.645\hat{\sigma}(t_0)]. \tag{B.5}$$

Estimate $\hat{G}(t_0)$ for the probability distribution $G(t_0)$ using a set of impostor scores $\mathbf{Y}$ can be obtained in a similar fashion. Parametric confidence intervals for this estimate can be calculated by replacing $\hat{F}(t_0)$ with $\hat{G}(t_0)$ and M with N in Equations (B.4) and (B.5).

Bibliography

[1] Online: http://svnext.it-sudparis.eu/svnview2-eph/ref_syst/. Cited on page(s) 95

[2] BioSecure Benchmarking Framework. http://svnext.it-sudparis.eu/svnview2-eph/ref_syst/. Cited on page(s) 94

[3] BioSecure Network of Excellence. www.biosecure.info. Cited on page(s) 95

[4] TURBINE – TrUsted Revocable Biometric IdeNtitiEs. Online: http://www.turbine-project.eu/. Cited on page(s) 1

[5] United States Visitor and Immigrant Status Indicator Technology (US-VISIT). Ofiicial website: http://www.dhs.gov/files/programs/usv.shtm. Cited on page(s) 4

[6] Advanced Encryption Standard (AES), November 2001. Cited on page(s) 6, 20

[7] Biosecure Tool: Performance Evaluation of A Biometric Verification System. Online: http://svnext.it-sudparis.eu/svnview2-eph/ref_syst/Tools/PerformanceEvaluation/doc/, 2007. Cited on page(s) 14, 15

[8] BIOmetrics and crypTographY for Fair aUthentication Licensing (BIOTYFUL). Agence Nationale de la Recherche (ANR), 2007–2010. ANR-06-TCOM-018. Cited on page(s) 1, 11

[9] Mohamed Abid and Hossam Afifi. Towards a Secure e-Passport Protocol based on Biometrics. *Journal of Information Assurance and Security (JIAS) (Special Issue on Access Control and Protocols)*, 4(4):338–345, 2009. Cited on page(s) 82, 83

[10] Mohamed Abid, Sanjay Kanade, Dijana Petrovska-Delacrétaz, Bernadette Dorizzi, and Hossam Afifi. Iris based Authentication Mechanism for e-Passports. In *2nd International Workshop on Security and Communication Networks (IWSCN)*, 2010. DOI: 10.1109/IWSCN.2010.5497990 Cited on page(s) 82

[11] Andy Adler. Sample Images Can be Independently Restored from Face Recognition Templates. In *Canadian Conference on Electrical and Computer Engineering (CCECE)*, 2003. DOI: 10.1109/CCECE.2003.1226104 Cited on page(s) 5, 19

[12] Gaurav Aggarwal, Nalini K. Ratha, Jonathan H. Connell, and Ruud M. Bolle. Physics based Revocable Face Recognition. In *International Conference on Acoustics, Speech, and Signal Processing (ICASSP)*, 2008. DOI: 10.1109/ICASSP.2008.4518839 Cited on page(s) 25

[13] Russell Ang, Rei Safavi-Naini, and Luke McAven. Cancelable Key-based Fingerprint Templates. In C. Boyd and J. M. González Neito, editors, *Proceedings of the 10th Australasian Conference on Information Security and Privacy*, pages 242–252, July 2005. Cited on page(s) 25

[14] Savvas Argyropoulos, Dimitrios Tzovaras, Dimosthenis Ioannidis, and Michael G. Strintzis. A Channel Coding Approach for Human Authentication From Gait Sequences. *IEEE Transactions on Information Forensics and Security*, 4(3):428 – 440, 2009. DOI: 10.1109/TIFS.2009.2025858 Cited on page(s) 46

[15] Lucas Ballard, Seny Kanmara, and Michael K. Reiter. The Practical Subtleties of Biometric Key generation. In *17th USENIX Security Symposium*, 2008. Cited on page(s) 51

[16] Mauro Barni, Tiziano Bianchi, Dario Catalano, Mario Di Raimondo, Ruggero Donida Labati, Pierluigi Failla, Dario Fiore, Riccardo Lazzeretti, Vincenzo Piuri, Fabio Scotti, and Alessandro Piva. Privacy-Preserving Fingercode Authentication. In *The 12th ACM Workshop on Multimedia and Security (MM&Sec10)*, Rome, Italy, Sept. 2010. DOI: 10.1145/1854229.1854270 Cited on page(s) 82, 83

[17] Claude Barral. *Biometrics & Security: Combining Fingerprints, Smart Cards and Cryptography*. Ph.D. thesis, Ecole Polytechnique Fédérale de Lausannel, June 2010. Cited on page(s) 21

[18] Rima Belguechi and Christophe Rosenberger. Study on the Convergence of Finger-Hashing and a Secured Biometric System. In *Proceedings of the Confrence Internationale sur l'Informatique et ses Application*, 2009. Cited on page(s) 24

[19] J. O. Berger. *A Stastical Decision Theory*. Springer-Verlag, 1980. Cited on page(s) 14

[20] J. R. Beveridge, D. Bolme, B. A. Raper, and M. Teixeira. The CSU Face Identification Evaluation System. *Machine Vision and Applications*, 16(2):128–138, 2005. DOI: 10.1007/s00138-004-0144-7 Cited on page(s) 97

[21] Vishnu Naresh Boddeti, Fei Su, and B.V.K. Vijaya Kumar. A Biometric Key-Binding and template Protection Framework Using Correlation Filters. In M. Tistarelli and M. Nixon, editors, *International Conference on Biometrics (ICB)*, pages 919–929, 2009. Cited on page(s) 51

[22] Ruud M. Bolle, Nalini K. Ratha, and Sharath Pankanti. Error Analysis of Pattern Recognition Systems – the Subsets Bootstrap. *Computer Vision and Image Understanding*, 93(1):1–33, January 2004. DOI: 10.1016/j.cviu.2003.08.002 Cited on page(s) 14, 101

[23] T. Boult. Robust Distance Measures for Face-Recognition Supporting Revocable Biometric Tokens. In *IEEE Conference on Automatic Face and Gesture Recognition (FG)*, 2006. DOI: 10.1109/FGR.2006.94 Cited on page(s) 24

[24] T. E. Boult, W. J. Scheirer, and R. Woodworth. Revocable Fingerprint Biotokens: Accuracy and Security Analysis. In *IEEE Conference on Computer Vision and Pattern Recognition*, pages 1–8, June 2007. DOI: 10.1109/CVPR.2007.383110 Cited on page(s) 24, 83

[25] Xavier Boyen. Reusable Cryptographic Fuzzy Extractors. In *11th ACM Conference on Computer and Communications Security (CCS)*, 2004. DOI: 10.1145/1030083.1030096 Cited on page(s) 49, 52, 81

[26] Xavier Boyen, Yevgeniy Dodis, Jonathan Katz, Rafail Ostrovsky, and Adam Smith. Secure Remote Authentication Using Biometric Data. In *Eurocrypt*, 2005. DOI: 10.1007/11426639_9 Cited on page(s) 81, 83

[27] J. Bringer, H. Chabanne, G. Cohen, B. Kindarji, and G. Zémor. Optimal Iris Fuzzy Sketches. In *IEEE Conference on Biometrics: Theory, Applications and Systems*, 2007. DOI: 10.1109/BTAS.2007.4401904 Cited on page(s) 50, 57

[28] Julien Bringer, Hervé Chabanne, Gerard Cohen, Bruno Kindarji, and Gilles Zémor. Theoretical and Practical Boundaries of Binary Secure Sketches. *IEEE Transactions on Information Forensics and Security*, 3(4):673–683, December 2008. DOI: 10.1109/TIFS.2008.2002937 Cited on page(s) 50

[29] Julien Bringer, Hervé Chabanne, Malika Izabachène, David Pointcheval, Qiang Tang, and Sébastien Zimmer. An Application of the Goldwasser-Micali Cryptosystem to Biometric Authentication. In *The 12th Australasian Conference on Information Security and Privacy (ACISP '07)*, 2007. DOI: 10.1007/978-3-540-73458-1_8 Cited on page(s) 82, 83

[30] Julien Bringer, Hervé Chabanne, and Bruno Kindarji. The Best of Both Worlds: Applying Secure Sketches to Cancelable Biometrics. *Science of Computer Programming*, 74(1–2):43–51, December 2008. DOI: 10.1016/j.scico.2008.09.016 Cited on page(s) 50

[31] Ileana Buhan. *Cryptographic Keys from Noisy Data*. Ph.D. thesis, University of Twente, Netherlands, 2008. Cited on page(s) 82

[32] Ileana Buhan, Jeroen Doumen, Pieter Hartel, and Raymond Veldhuis. Secure Ad-hoc Pairing with Biometrics: SAfE. Technical Report, University of Twente, 2007. DOI: 10.1504/IJSN.2009.023424 Cited on page(s) 82

[33] Francis Minhthang Bui, Karl Martin, Haiping Lu, Konstantinos N. Plataniotis, and Dimitrios Hatzinakos. Fuzzy Key Binding Strategies based on Quantization Index Modulation (QIM) for Biometric Encryption (BE) Applications. *IEEE Transactions on Information Forensics and Security*, 5(1):118–132, 2010. DOI: 10.1109/TIFS.2009.2037662 Cited on page(s) 50

[34] William E. Burr, Donna F. Dodson, and W. Timothy Polk. Electronic Authentication Guideline: Recommendations of the National Institute of Standards and Technology, April 2006. Cited on page(s) 64

[35] Anne M. P. Canuto, Fernando Pintro, Antonino Feitosa Neto, and Michael C. Fairhurst. Enhancing Performance of Cancellable Fingerprint Biometrics Using Classifier Ensembles. In *Eleventh Brazilian Symposium on Neural Networks (SBRN)*, 2010. DOI: 10.1109/SBRN.2010.18 Cited on page(s) 24

[36] R. Cappelli, A. Lumini, D. Maio, and D. Maltoni. Can Fingerprints be Reconstructed from ISO Templates? In *9th International Conference on Control, Automation, Robotics and Vision (ICARCV)*, 2006. DOI: 10.1109/ICARCV.2006.345478 Cited on page(s) 5, 19

[37] R. Cappelli, D. Maio, A. Lumini, and D. Maltoni. Fingerprint Image Reconstruction from Standard Templates. *IEEE Transactions on Pattern Analysis and Machine Intelligence*, 29(9):1489–1503, September 2007. DOI: 10.1109/TPAMI.2007.1087 Cited on page(s) 5, 19

[38] Ann Cavoukian and Alex Stoianov. Biometric Encryption: A Positive-sum Technology that Achieves Strong Authentication, Security and Privacy. White paper, Information and Privacy commissioner of Ontario, March 2007. Cited on page(s) 10

[39] Ee-Chien Chang and Qiming Li. Hiding Secret Points amidst Chaff. In *Proceedings of the Eurocrypt 2006*, 2006. DOI: 10.1007/11761679_5 Cited on page(s) 51

[40] Yuo-Jen Chang, Wende Zhung, and Tsiihun Chen. Biometrics-based Cryptographic Key Generation. In *IEEE International Conference on Multimedia and Expo (ICME)*, volume 3, pages 2203–2206, June 2004. DOI: 10.1109/ICME.2004.1394707 Cited on page(s) 51

[41] C. Chen, R.N.J. Veldhuis, T.A.M. Kevenaar, and A.H.M. Akkermans. Biometric Binary String Generation with Detection Rate Optimized Bit Allocation. In *IEEE Conference on Computer Vision and Pattern Recognition Workshops*, 2008. DOI: 10.1109/CVPRW.2008.4563112 Cited on page(s) 97

[42] Sharat Chikkerur, Nalini K. Ratha, Jonathan H. Connell, and Ruud M. Bolle. Generating Registration-free Cancelable Fingerprint Templates. In *IEEE International Conference on Biometrics: Theory, Applications and Systems*, 2008. DOI: 10.1109/BTAS.2008.4699375 Cited on page(s) 25

[43] Chong Siew Chin, Andrew Teoh Beng Jin, and David Ngo Chek Ling. High Security Iris Verification System based on Random Secret Integration. *Computer Vision and Image Understanding*, 102(2):169–177, 2006. DOI: 10.1016/j.cviu.2006.01.002 Cited on page(s) 25

[44] Stelvio Cimato, Marco Gamassi, Vincenzo Piuri, Roberto Sassi, and Fabio Scotti. Privacy-Aware Biometrics: Design and Implementation of a Multimodal Verification System. In *Annual Computer Security Applications Conference (ACSAC)*, 2008. DOI: 10.1109/ACSAC.2008.13 Cited on page(s) 52

[45] T. Charles Clancy, Negar Kiyavash, and Dennis J. Lin. Secure Smartcard-based Fingerprint Authentication. In *Proceeding of ACM SIGMM Workshop on Biometrics Methods and Applications*, pages 45–52, November 2003. DOI: 10.1145/982507.982516 Cited on page(s) 49

[46] Tee Connie, Andrew Teoh, Michael Goh, and David Ngo. Palmhashing: A Novel Approach for Cancelable Biometrics. *Information Processing Letters*, 93(1):1–5, January 2005. DOI: 10.1016/j.ipl.2004.09.014 Cited on page(s) 25

[47] John Daugman. The Importance of Being Random: Statistical Principles of Iris Recognition. *Pattern Recognition*, 36(2):279–291, February 2003. DOI: 10.1016/S0031-3203(02)00030-4 Cited on page(s) 64, 70

[48] John Daugman. How Iris Recognition Works. *IEEE Transactions on Circuits and Systems for Video Technology*, 14:21–30, January 2004. DOI: 10.1109/TCSVT.2003.818350 Cited on page(s) 95

[49] G. I. Davida, Y. Frankel, and B. J. Matt. On Enabling Secure Applications through Off-line Biometric Identification. In *Proceedings of the IEEE Symposium on Privacy and Security*, pages 148–157, 1998. DOI: 10.1109/SECPRI.1998.674831 Cited on page(s) 1, 44, 46

[50] G. I. Davida, Y. Frankel, B. J. Matt, and R. Peralta. On the Relation of Error Correction and Cryptography to an Offline Biometric based Identification Scheme. In *Proceedings Workshop on Coding and Cryptography*, pages 129–138, 1999. Cited on page(s)

[51] T. Dierks and C. Allen. The TLS Protocol, Version 1.0. Request for Comments: 2246, Internet Engineering Task Force (IETF), January 1999. Cited on page(s) 8

[52] T. Dierks and E. Rescorla. The Transport Layer Security (TLS) Protocol Version 1.2. Request for Comments: 5246, Internet Engineering Task Force (IETF), August 2008. Cited on page(s) 8, 80, 83

[53] Whitfield Diffie and Martin Hellman. New Directions in Cryptography. *IEEE Transactions on Information Theory*, 22(6):644–654, 1976. DOI: 10.1109/TIT.1976.1055638 Cited on page(s) 7

[54] Y. Dodis, L. Reyzin, and A. Smith. Fuzzy extractors: How to Generate Strong Keys from Biometrics and Other Noisy Data. In *Proceedings of the Eurocrypt 2004*, pages 523–540, 2004. DOI: 10.1137/060651380 Cited on page(s) 49, 52

[55] Taher Elgamal. A Public Key Cryptosystem and a Signature Scheme based on Discrete Logarithms. *IEEE Transactions on Information Theory*, 31(4):469 – 472, 1985. DOI: 10.1109/TIT.1985.1057074 Cited on page(s) 82

[56] Zekeriya Erkin, Martin Franz, Jorge Guajardo, Stefan Katzenbeisser, Inald Lagendijk, and Tomas Toft. Privacy-Preserving Face Recognition. In I. Goldberg and M. Atallah, editors, *Proceedings of 9th International Syposium on Privacy Enhancing Technologies*, 2009. DOI: 10.1007/978-3-642-03168-7 Cited on page(s) 82

[57] Chun-I Fan and Yi-Hui Lin. Provably Secure Remote Truly Three-Factor Authentication Scheme With Privacy Protection on Biometrics. *IEEE Transactions on Information Forensics and Security*, 4(4):933–945, December 2009. DOI: 10.1109/TIFS.2009.2031942 Cited on page(s) 82

[58] Faisal Farooq, Ruud M. Bolle, Tsai-Yang Jea, and Nalini Ratha. Anonymous and Revocable Fingerprint Recognition. In *IEEE Conference on Computer Vision and Pattern Recognition (CVPR)*, 2007. DOI: 10.1109/CVPR.2007.383382 Cited on page(s) 25, 31

[59] Yi C. Feng, Pong C. Yuen, and Anil K. Jain. A Hybrid Approach for Generating Secure and Discriminating Face Template. *IEEE Transactions on Information Forensics and Security*, 5(1):103 –117, March 2010. DOI: 10.1109/TIFS.2009.2038760 Cited on page(s) 50

[60] Manuel R. Freire, Julian Fierrez, and Javier Ortega-Garcia. Dynamic Signature Verification with Template Protection Using Helper Data. In *International Conference on Acaustics, Speech, and Signal Processing (ICASSP)*, 2008. DOI: 10.1109/ICASSP.2008.4517959 Cited on page(s) 50

[61] Bo Fu, Simon X. Yang, Jianping Li, and Dekun Hu. Multibiometric Cryptosystem: Model Structure and Performance Analysis. *IEEE Transactions on Information Forensics and Security*, 4(4):867–882, 2009. DOI: 10.1109/TIFS.2009.2033227 Cited on page(s) 52

[62] Alwyn Goh and David C.L. Ngo. Computation of Cryptographic Keys from Face Biometrics. In A. Lioy and D. Mazzocchi, editors, *Proceedings of the International Federation for Information Processing*, volume 2828 of *Lecture Notes in Computer Science*, pages 1–13. Springer Berlin / Heidelberg, 2003. Cited on page(s) 23, 46

[63] Shafi Goldwasser and Silvio Micali. Probabilistic Encryption and How to Play Mental Poker Keeping Secret All Partial Information. In *Proceedings of the Fourteenth Annual ACM Symposium on Theory of Computing*, 1982. DOI: 10.1145/800070.802212 Cited on page(s) 82

[64] Feng Hao. *On Using Fuzzy Data in Security Mechanisms*. Ph.D. thesis, Queens College, Cambridge, April 2007. Cited on page(s) 49

[65] Feng Hao, Ross Anderson, and John Daugman. Combining Crypto with Biometrics Effectively. *IEEE Transactions on Computers*, 55(9):1081–1088, 2006. DOI: 10.1109/TC.2006.138 Cited on page(s) viii, 16, 41, 49, 50, 52, 53, 54, 55, 57, 59, 60, 61, 64

[66] Feng Hao and Choong Wah Chan. Private Key Generation from On-line Handwritten Signatures. *Information Management and Computer Security*, 10(4):159–164, 2002. DOI: 10.1108/09685220210436949 Cited on page(s) 46

[67] Tanya Ignatenko and Frans M. J. Willems. Biometric Systems: Privacy and Secrecy Aspects. *IEEE Transactions on Information Forensics and Security*, 4(4):956–973, December 2009. DOI: 10.1109/TIFS.2009.2033228 Cited on page(s) 51

[68] ISO/IEC 24745. Information Technology – Security Techniques – Biometric Information Protection, 2011. Cited on page(s) 1

[69] ISO/IEC CD 2382.37. Information Processing Systems Vocabulary Part 37 : Harmonized Biometric Vocabulary, 2010. Cited on page(s) 2

[70] Y. Itakura and S. Tsujii. Proposal on a Multifactor Biometric Authentication Method based on Cryptosystem Keys Containing Biometric Signatures. *International Journal of Information Security*, pages 288–296, 2005. DOI: 10.1007/s10207-004-0065-5 Cited on page(s) 42

[71] Anil K. Jain, Karthik Nandakumar, and Abhishek Nagar. Biometric template security. *EURASIP Journal on Advances in Signal Processing*, 2008 (Article ID 579416):17 pages. DOI: 10.1155/2008/579416 Cited on page(s) 10, 47

[72] Jason Jeffers and Arathi Arakala. Minutiae-based Structures for A Fuzzy Vault. In *Biometrics Symposium (BSYM)*, 2006. Cited on page(s) 51

[73] Andrew Teoh Beng Jin and Tee Connie. Remarks on Biohashing based Cancelable Biometrics in Verification System. *Neurocomputing*, 69(16-18):2461–2464, October 2006. Brain Inspired Cognitive Systems - Selected papers from the 1st International Conference on Brain Inspired Cognitive Systems (BICS 2004). DOI: 10.1016/j.neucom.2006.01.024 Cited on page(s) 24

[74] Andrew Teoh Beng Jin, David Ngo, Chek Ling, and Alwyn Goh. Biohashing: Two Factor Authentication Featuring Fingerprint Data and Tokenised Random Number. *Pattern Recognition*, 37(11):2245–2255, November 2004. DOI: 10.1016/j.patcog.2004.04.011 Cited on page(s) 23, 24, 46

[75] A. Juels and M. Sudan. A Fuzzy Vault Scheme. In A. Lapidoth and E. Teletar, editors, *Proc. IEEE Int. Symp. Information Theory*, page 408. IEEE Press, 2002. Cited on page(s) 49, 83

[76] A. Juels and M. Wattenberg. A Fuzzy Commitment Scheme. In *Proceedings of the Sixth ACM Conference on Computer and communication Security (CCCS)*, pages 28–36, 1999. DOI: 10.1145/319709.319714 Cited on page(s) 41, 49, 53, 97

[77] Sanjay Kanade, Danielle Camara, Emine Krichen, Dijana Petrovska-Delacrétaz, and Bernadette Dorizzi. Three Factor Scheme for Biometric-based Cryptographic Key Regeneration Using Iris. In *The 6th Biometrics Symposium (BSYM)*, September 2008. DOI: 10.1109/BSYM.2008.4655523 Cited on page(s) 19, 52, 82

[78] Sanjay Kanade, Emine Krichen, Dijana Petrovska-Delacrétaz, and Bernadette Dorizzi. Three Factor Scheme for Biometric-based Cryptographic Key Regeneration Using Iris. Technical report, Institut TELECOM: TELECOM SudParis, 2008. DOI: 10.1109/BSYM.2008.4655523 Cited on page(s) 44

[79] Sanjay Kanade, Dijana Petrovska-Delacrétaz, and Bernadette Dorizzi. Cancelable Iris Biometrics and Using Error Correcting Codes to Reduce Variability in Biometric Data. In *IEEE Computer Society Conference on Computer Vision and Pattern Recognition*, June 2009. DOI: 10.1109/CVPRW.2009.5206646 Cited on page(s)

[80] Sanjay Kanade, Dijana Petrovska-Delacrétaz, and Bernadette Dorizzi. Multi-Biometrics based Cryptographic Key Regeneration Scheme. In *IEEE International Conference on Biometrics: Theory, Applications, and Systems (BTAS)*, September 2009. DOI: 10.1109/BTAS.2009.5339034 Cited on page(s)

[81] Sanjay Kanade, Dijana Petrovska-Delacrétaz, and Bernadette Dorizzi. Generating and Sharing Biometrics based Session Keys for Secure Cryptographic Applications. In *IEEE International Conference on Biometrics: Theory, Applications, and Systems (BTAS)*, 2010. DOI: 10.1109/BTAS.2010.5634545 Cited on page(s) 80

[82] Sanjay Kanade, Dijana Petrovska-Delacrétaz, and Bernadette Dorizzi. Obtaining Cryptographic Keys Using Feature Level Fusion of Iris and Face Biometrics for Secure User Authentication. In *IEEE CVPR Workshop on Biometrics*, June 2010. DOI: 10.1109/CVPRW.2010.5544618 Cited on page(s)

[83] Sanjay Kanade, Dijana Petrovska-Delacrétaz, and Bernadette Dorizzi. Multi-biometrics based Crypto-biometric Session Key Generation and Sharing Protocol. In *ACM Workshop on Mumtimedia and Security (MM&Sec)*, 2011. DOI: 10.1145/2037252.2037272 Cited on page(s) 81

[84] Sanjay Ganesh Kanade. *Enhancing Information Security and Privacy by Combining Biometrics with Cryptography*. Ph.D. thesis, TELECOM & Management SudParis and l'Université d'Évry-Val d'Essonne, Evry, France, 2010. Cited on page(s) 52

[85] E. J. C. Kelkboom, B. Gökberk, T. A. M. Kevenaar, A. H. M. Akkermans, and M. van der Veen. "3D Face": Biometric Template Protection for 3D Face Recognition. In *International Conference on Biometrics*, 2007. DOI: 10.1007/978-3-540-74549-5_60 Cited on page(s) 50, 97

[86] E.J.C. Kelkboom, X. Zhou, J. Breebaart, R.N.J. Veldhuis, and C. Busch. Multi-Algorithm Fusion with Template Protection. In *IEEE Second International Conference on Biometrics Theory, Applications and Systems*, 2009. Cited on page(s) 52

[87] Emile J. C. Kelkboom, Jeroen Breebaart, Tom A. M. Kevenaar, Ileana Buhan, and Raymond N. J. Veldhuis. Preventing the Decodability Attack based Cross-Matching in a Fuzzy Commitment Scheme. *IEEE Transactions on Information Forensics and Security*, 6(1):107–121, March 2011. DOI: 10.1109/TIFS.2010.2091637 Cited on page(s) 50

[88] Auguste Kerckhoffs. La Cryptographie Militaire. *Journal des Sciences Militaires*, 9:5–38, January, 161–191, February 1883. Cited on page(s) 9, 79

[89] T.A.M. Kevenaar, G.J. Schrijen, M. van der Veen, A.H.M. Akkermans, and F. Zuo. Face Recognition with Renewable and Privacy Preserving Binary Templates. In *Fourth IEEE Workshop on Automatic Identification Advanced Technologies*, October 2005. DOI: 10.1109/AUTOID.2005.24 Cited on page(s) 50, 97

[90] Neal Koblitz. Elliptic Curve Cryptosystems. *Mathematics of Computation*, 48:203–209, 1987. DOI: 10.1090/S0025-5718-1987-0866109-5 Cited on page(s) 7

[91] Adams Kong, King-Hong Cheung, David Zhang, Mohamed Kamel, and Jane You. An Analysis of Biohashing and its Variants. *Pattern Recognition*, 39(7):1359–1368, July 2006. DOI: 10.1016/j.patcog.2005.10.025 Cited on page(s) 24

[92] Peter Kovesi. Matlab and Octave Functions for Computer Vision and Image Processing. Online: http://www.csse.uwa.edu.au/$\sim$pk/Research/MatlabFns/, 2005. Cited on page(s) 97

[93] Emine Krichen, Bernadette Dorizzi, Zhenan Sun, Sonia Garcia-Salicetti, and Tieniu Tan. Iris Recognition. In Dijana Petrovska-Delacrétaz, Gérard Chollet, and Bernadette Dorizzi, editors, *Guide to Biometric Reference Systems and Performance Evaluation*, pages 25–50. Springer-Verlag, 2009. DOI: 10.1007/978-1-84800-292-0 Cited on page(s) 95, 98

[94] Amioy Kumar and Ajay Kumar. Development of a New Cryptographic Construct Using Palmprint-based Fuzzy Vault. *EURASIP Journal on Advances in Signal Processing*, 2009:11, 2009. DOI: 10.1155/2009/967046 Cited on page(s) 51

[95] Martin Lades, Jan C. Vorbrüuggen, Joachim Buhmann, Jöorg Lange, Christoph v.d. Malsburg, Rolf P. Wüurtz, and Wolfgang Konen. Distortion Invariant Object Recognition in the Dynamic Link Architecture. *IEEE Transactions on Computers*, 42(3):300–311, March 1993. DOI: 10.1109/12.210173 Cited on page(s) 97

[96] Lifeng Lai, Siu-Wai Ho, and H. Vincent Poor. Privacy Security Trade-Offs in Biometric Security Systems Part I: Single Use Case. *IEEE Transactions on Information Forensics and*

Security, 6(1):122–139, March 2011. DOI: 10.1109/TIFS.2010.2098873 Cited on page(s) 51

[97] Lifeng Lai, Siu-Wai Ho, and H. Vincent Poor. Privacy Security Trade-Offs in Biometric Security Systems Part II: Multiple Use Case. *IEEE Transactions on Information Forensics and Security*, 6(1):140–151, March 2011. DOI: 10.1109/TIFS.2010.2098873 Cited on page(s) 51

[98] Chulhan Lee, Jeung-Yoon Cho, Kar-Ann Toh, Sangyoun Lee, and Jaihie Kim. Alignment-free Cancelable Fingerprint Templates based on Local Minutiae Information. *IEEE Transactions on Systems, Man, and Cybernetics–Part B: Cybernetics*, 34(4):980–992, August 2007. DOI: 10.1109/TSMCB.2007.896999 Cited on page(s) 25

[99] Peng Li, Xin Yang, Kai Cao, Xunqiang Tao, Ruifang Wang, and Jie Tian. An Aalignment-Free Fingerprint Cryptosystem based on Fuzzy Vault Scheme. *Journal of Network and Computer Applications*, 33:207–220, 2010. DOI: 10.1016/j.jnca.2009.12.003 Cited on page(s) 25, 51

[100] Qiming Li, Muchuan Guo, and Ee-Chien Chang. Fuzzy Extractors for Asymmetric Biometric Representations. In *IEEE Computer Society Conference on Computer Vision and Pattern Recognition Workshops, (CVPRW '08)*, pages 1–6, June 2008. DOI: 10.1109/CVPRW.2008.4563113 Cited on page(s) 51

[101] Qiming Li, Yagiz Sutcu, and Nasir Memon. Secure Sketch for Biometric Templates. In *Asiacrypt*, December 2006. DOI: 10.1007/11935230_7 Cited on page(s) 51

[102] Alessandra Lumini and Loris Nanni. An Improved Biohashing for Human Authentication. *Pattern Recognition*, 40(3):1057–1065, March 2007. DOI: 10.1016/j.patcog.2006.05.030 Cited on page(s) 23

[103] Ying Luo, Sen ching S. Cheung, and Shuiming Ye. Anonymous Biometric Access Control based on Homomorphic Encryption. In *IEEE International Conference on Multimedia and Expo (ICME)*, 2009. DOI: 10.1109/ICME.2009.5202677 Cited on page(s) 82

[104] F. J. MacWilliams and N. J. A. Sloane. *Theory of Error-Correcting Codes*. North Holland, 1991. Cited on page(s) 16, 55, 56, 64, 67

[105] E. Maiorana, M. Martinez-Diaz, P. Campisi, J. Ortega-Garcia, and A. Neri. Template Protection for HMM-based On-line Signature Authentication. In *IEEE CVPR Workshop on Biometrics*, 2008. DOI: 10.1109/CVPRW.2008.4563114 Cited on page(s) 24

[106] Emanuele Maiorana and Patrizio Campisi. Fuzzy Commitment for Function based Signature Template Protection. *IEEE Signal Processing Letters*, 17(3):249 – 252, 2010. DOI: 10.1109/LSP.2009.2038111 Cited on page(s) 51

[107] Emanuele Maiorana, Patrizio Campisi, Julian Fierrez, Javier Ortega-Garcia, and Alessandro Neri. Cancelable Templates for Sequence based Biometrics with Application to On-line Signature Recognition. *IEEE Transactions on Systems, Man and Cybernetics, Part A: Systems and Humans*, 40(3):525–538, 2010. DOI: 10.1109/TSMCA.2010.2041653 Cited on page(s) 24

[108] Emanuele Maiorana, Patrizio Campisi, and Alessandro Neri. User Adaptive Fuzzy Commitment for Signature Template Protection and Renewability. *Jounal of Electronic Imaging*, 17(1), 2008. DOI: 10.1117/1.2885239 Cited on page(s) 50

[109] Emanuele Maiorana, Patrizio Campisi, and Alessandro Neri. Bioconvolving: Cancelable Templates for a Multi-Biometrics Signature Recognition System. In *IEEE International Systems Conference (SysCon)*, 2011. DOI: 10.1109/SYSCON.2011.5929064 Cited on page(s) 24

[110] Emanuele Maiorana, Patrizio Campisi, Javier Ortega-Garcia, and Alessandro Neri. Cancelable Biometrics for HMM-based Signature Recognition. In *IEEE Conference on Biometrics: Theory, Applications and Systems (BTAS)*, 2008. DOI: 10.1109/BTAS.2008.4699360 Cited on page(s) 24

[111] Wenbo Mao. *Modern Cryptography: Theory and Practice*. Prentice Hall, August 2003. Cited on page(s) 79

[112] A. Martin, G. Doddington, T. Kamm, M. Ordowski, and M. Przybocki. The DET Curve in Assessment of Detection Task Performance. In *Proceedings of the Eurospeech*, 1997. Cited on page(s) 14

[113] Microsoft Corporation. Windows Biometric Framework – Guidelines for IHV, ISVs and OEMs. Online, March 19, 2009. http://www.microsoft.com/whdc/Device/biometric/WBFIntro.mspx. Cited on page(s) 43

[114] Preda Mihăilescu. The Fuzzy Vault for Fingerprints is Vulnerable to Brute Force Attack. Online, 2007. http://arxiv.org/abs/0708.2974v1. Cited on page(s) 51

[115] Victor Miller. Use of Elliptic Curves in Cryptography. In *Advances in Cryptology (CRYPTO '85)*, 1986. Cited on page(s) 7

[116] F. Monrose, M.K. Reiter, Qi Li, and S. Wetzel. Cryptographic Key Generation from Voice. In *Proceedings of the IEEE Symposium on Security and Privacy*, pages 202–213, May 2001. DOI: 10.1109/SECPRI.2001.924299 Cited on page(s) 44

[117] F. Monrose, M.K. Reiter, and R. Wetzel. Password Hardening based on Keystroke Dynamics. In *Proceedings of the Sixth ACM Conference on Computer and communication Security (CCCS)*, pages 73–82, 1999. DOI: 10.1145/319709.319720 Cited on page(s) 44

[118] Abhishek Nagar and Santanu Chaudhury. Biometrics based Asymmetric Cryptosystem Design Using. Modified Fuzzy Vault Scheme. In *18th International Conference on Pattern Recognition (ICPR)*, 2006. DOI: 10.1109/ICPR.2006.330 Cited on page(s) 51

[119] Abhishek Nagar, Karthik Nandakumar, and Anil K. Jain. Securing Fingerprint Template: Fuzzy Vault with Minutiae Descriptors. In *International Conference on Pattern Recognition (ICPR)*, pages 1–4, 2008. DOI: 10.1109/ICPR.2008.4761459 Cited on page(s) 52

[120] Abhishek Nagar and Anil K. Jain. On the Security of Non-Invertible Fingerprint Template Transforms. In *IEEE International Workshop on Information Forensics and Security*, December 2009. Cited on page(s) 51

[121] Abhishek Nagar, Karthik Nandakumar, and Anil K. Jain. A Hybrid Biometric Cryptosystem for Securing Fingerprint Minutiae Templates. *Pattern Recognition Letters*, 31(8):733–741, 2009. DOI: 10.1016/j.patrec.2009.07.003 Cited on page(s) 52

[122] Karthik Nandakumar. *Multibiometric Systems: Fusion Strategies and Template Security*. Ph.D. thesis, Department of Computer Science and Engineering, Michigan State University, 2008. Cited on page(s) 51, 52

[123] Karthik Nandakumar. A Fingerprint Cryptosystem based on Minutiae Phase Spectrum. In *IEEE International Workshop on Information Forensics and Security (WIFS)*, 2010. DOI: 10.1109/WIFS.2010.5711456 Cited on page(s) 51

[124] Karthik Nandakumar and Anil K. Jain. Multibiometric Template Security using Fuzzy Vault. In *IEEE Second International Conference on Biometrics: Theory, Applications and Systems*, 2008. DOI: 10.1109/BTAS.2008.4699352 Cited on page(s) 51, 52

[125] Karthik Nandakumar, Anil K. Jain, and Sharath Pankanti. Fingerprint-based Fuzzy Vault: Implementation and Performance. *IEEE Transactions of Information Forensics and Security*, 2(4):744–757, December 2007. DOI: 10.1109/TIFS.2007.908165 Cited on page(s) 49, 52

[126] Karthik Nandakumar, Abhishek Nagar, and Anil K. Jain. Hardening Fingerprint Fuzzy Vault Using Password. In *Proceedings of the International Conference on Biometrics*, 2007. DOI: 10.1007/978-3-540-74549-5_97 Cited on page(s) 50, 51

[127] Loris Nanni and Alessandra Lumini. Random Subspace for an Improved BioHashing for Face Authentication. *Pattern Recognition Letters*, 29:295–300, 2008. DOI: 10.1016/j.patrec.2007.10.005 Cited on page(s) 24

[128] Loris Nanni and Alessandra Lumini. Empirical Tests on BioHashing. *Neurocomputing*, 69:2390–2395, 2006. DOI: 10.1016/j.neucom.2006.05.001 Cited on page(s) 24

[129] Loris Nanni, Emanuele Maiorana, Alessandra Lumini, and Patrizio Campisi. Combining Local, Regional and Global Matchers for a Template Protected On-line Signature Verification System. *Expert Systems with Applications*, 37:3676–3684, 2010. DOI: 10.1016/j.eswa.2009.10.023 Cited on page(s) 24

[130] National Institute of Science and Technology (NIST). Face Recognition Grand Challenge, 2005. http://www.frvt.org/FRGC/. Cited on page(s) 27, 34, 66, 99

[131] National Institute of Science and Technology (NIST). Iris Challenge Evaluation, 2005. http://iris.nist.gov/ice. Cited on page(s) 27, 30, 32, 33, 34, 57, 62, 63, 98

[132] Dijana Petrovska-Delacrétaz, Gérard Chollet, and Bernadette Dorizzi, editors. *Guide to Biometric Reference Systems and Performance Evaluation*. Springer-Verlag, 2009. DOI: 10.1007/978-1-84800-292-0 Cited on page(s) 14, 15, 27, 29, 30, 57, 58, 62, 97, 101

[133] P. Jonathon Phillips, Patrick J. Flynn, Todd Scruggs, Kevin W. Bowyer, Jin Chang, Kevin Hoffman, Joe Marques, Jaesik Min, and William Worek. Overview of the Face Recognition Grand Challenge. In *IEEE Computer Society Conference on Computer Vision and Pattern Recognition*, 2005. DOI: 10.1109/CVPR.2005.268 Cited on page(s) 99

[134] N. K. Ratha, J. H. Connell, and R. M. Bolle. Enhancing Security and Privacy in Biometrics-based Authentication Systems. *IBM Systems Journal*, 40(3):614–634, 2001. DOI: 10.1147/sj.403.0614 Cited on page(s) 23

[135] Nalini Ratha, Jonathan Connell, Ruud M. Bolle, and Sharat Chikkerur. Cancelable Biometrics: A Case Study in Fingerprints. In *18th International Conference on Pattern Recognition. (ICPR 2006)*, volume 4, pages 370–373, 2006. DOI: 10.1109/ICPR.2006.353 Cited on page(s) 23

[136] Nalini K. Ratha, Sharat Chikkerur, Jonathan H. Connell, and Ruud M. Bolle. Generating Cancelable Fingerprint Templates. *IEEE Transactions on Pattern Analysis and Machine Intelligence*, 29(4):561–572, April 2007. DOI: 10.1109/TPAMI.2007.1004 Cited on page(s) 23

[137] Christian Rathgeb and Andreas Uhl. A Survey on Biometric Cryptosystems and Cancelable Biometrics. *EURASIP Journal on Information Security*, 2011(3):1–25, 2011. DOI: 10.1186/1687-417X-2011-3 Cited on page(s) 10

[138] Christian Rathgeb and Andreas Uhl. Statistical Attack against Iris-Biometric Fuzzy Commitment Schemes. In *CVPR Workshop on Biometrics,*, pages 25–32, 2011. DOI: 10.1109/CVPRW.2011.5981720 Cited on page(s) 51

[139] Ronald Rivest, Adi Shamir, and Len Adleman. A Method for Obtaining Digital Signatures and Public-key Cryptosystems. *Communications of the ACM*, 21(2):120–126, 1978. DOI: 10.1145/359340.359342 Cited on page(s) 7

[140] A. Ross and A. K. Jain. Multimodal Biometrics: an Overview. In *Proceedings of the 12th European Signal Processing Conference (EUSIPCO)*, pages 1221–1224, September 2004. Cited on page(s) 51

[141] Arun Ross. An Introduction to Multibiometrics. In *Proceedings of the 15th Eurpoean Signal Processing Conference (EUSIPCO)*, 2007. DOI: 10.1007/978-0-387-71041-9_14 Cited on page(s) 51

[142] Arun Ross and Asem Othman. Visual Cryptography for Biometric Privacy. *IEEE Transactions on Information Forensics and Security*, 6(1):70–81, March 2011. DOI: 10.1109/TIFS.2010.2097252 Cited on page(s) 24

[143] Arun Ross, Jidnya Shah, and Anil K. Jain. From Template to Image: Reconstructing Fingerprints from Minutiae Points. *IEEE Transactions on Pattern Analysis and Machine Intelligence*, 29(4):544–560, April 2007. DOI: 10.1109/TPAMI.2007.1018 Cited on page(s) 5, 19

[144] Arun Ross, Samir Shah, and Jidnya Shah. Image Versus Feature Mosaicing: A Case Study in Fingerprints. In *SPIE Conference on Biometric Technology for Human Identification*, 2006. DOI: 10.1117/12.666278 Cited on page(s) 49

[145] Arun A. Ross, Karthik Nandakumar, and Anil K. Jain. *Handbook of Multibiometrics*. International Series on Biometrics. Springer, 2006. Cited on page(s) 3, 51

[146] A. Sahai and B. Waters. Fuzzy Identity-based Encryption. In *EUROCRYPT*, pages 457–473, 2005. Cited on page(s) 49

[147] Marios Savvides, B.V.K. Vijaya Kumar, and P.K. Khosla. Cancelable Biometric Filters for Face Recognition. In *Proceedings of the 17th International Conference on Pattern Recognition (ICPR 04)*, volume 3, pages 922–925, August 2004. DOI: 10.1109/ICPR.2004.1334679 Cited on page(s) 24, 51

[148] Tobias Scheidat, Claus Vielhauer, and Jana Dittmann. Advanced Studies on Reproducibility of Biometric Hashes. In B. Schouten et al., editor, *Biometrics and Identity Management (BIOID)*, 2008. Cited on page(s) 15, 46

[149] W. J. Scheirer and T. E. Boult. Bio-Cryptographic Protocols with Bipartite Biotokens. In *Biometric Symposium*, 2008. DOI: 10.1109/BSYM.2008.4655516 Cited on page(s) 83

[150] W. J. Scheirer and T. E. Boult. Bipartite Biotokens: Definitions, Implementation, and Analysis. In *International Conference on Biometrics (ICB)*, 2009. DOI: 10.1007/978-3-642-01793-3_79 Cited on page(s) 83

[151] Walter J. Scheirer and Terrance E. Boult. Cracking Fuzzy Vaults and Biometric Encryption. In *Biometrics Symposium*, 2007. Cited on page(s) 49, 51

[152] Weiguo Sheng, Gareth Howells, Michael Fairhurst, and Farzin Deravi. Template-free Biometric-key Generation by Means of Fuzzy Genetic Clustering. *IEEE Transactions on Information Forensics and Security*, 3(2):183–191, June 2008. DOI: 10.1109/TIFS.2008.922056 Cited on page(s) 46

[153] Bernard Sklar. Reed-solomon codes. Available online (16 June 2010). www.phptr.com/content/images/art_sklar7_reed-solomon/elementLinks/art_sklar7_reed-solomon.pdf. Cited on page(s) 56

[154] C. Soutar, D. Roberge, A. Stoianov, R. Gilroy, and B.V.K. Vijaya Kumar. Biometric Encryption. In *ICSA guide to Cryptography*. McGraw-Hill, 1999. Cited on page(s) 47, 49

[155] A. Stoianov, T. Kevenaar, and M. van der Veen. Security Issues of Biometric Encryption. In *IEEE Toronto International Conference Science and Technology for Humanity (TIC-STH)*, 2009. DOI: 10.1109/TIC-STH.2009.5444478 Cited on page(s) 51, 66

[156] Alex Stoianov. Security of Error Correcting Code for Biometric Encryption (critical note). In *Eighth Annual International Conference on Privacy, Security and Trust*, 2010. DOI: 10.1109/PST.2010.5593246 Cited on page(s) 51

[157] Y. Sutcu, Qiming Li, and N. Memon. Secure Biometric Templates from Fingerprint-face Features. In *IEEE Conference on Computer Vision and Pattern Recognition, 2007*, pages 1–6, June 2007. DOI: 10.1109/CVPR.2007.383385 Cited on page(s) 51

[158] Yagiz Sutcu, Qiming Li, and Nasir Memon. Protecting Biometric Templates with Sketch: Theory and Practice. *IEEE Transactions on Information Forensics and Security*, 2(3):503–512, September 2007. DOI: 10.1109/TIFS.2007.902022 Cited on page(s) 50

[159] Qiang Tang, Julien Bringer, Hervé Chabanne, and David Pointcheval. A Formal Study of the Privacy Concerns in Biometric-based Remote Authentication Schemes. In *Information Security Practice and Experience Conference (ISPEC)*, 2008. DOI: 10.1007/978-3-540-79104-1_5 Cited on page(s) 82, 83

[160] Andrew Beng Jin Teoh and Chong Tze Yuang. Cancelable Biometrics Realization with Multispace Random Projections. *IEEE Transactions on Systems, Man, and Cybernetics, Part B-Cybernetics*, 37(5):1096–1106, October 2007. DOI: 10.1109/TSMCB.2007.903538 Cited on page(s) 24

[161] Andrew B.J. Teoh, Alwyn Goh, and David C.L. Ngo. Random Multispace Quantization as an Analytic Mechanism for BioHashing of Biometric and Random Identity Inputs. *IEEE Transactions on Pattern Analysis and Machine Intelligence*, 28(12):1892–1901, December 2006. DOI: 10.1109/TPAMI.2006.250 Cited on page(s) 24

[162] Andrew B.J. Teoh, Yip Wai Kuan, and Sangyoun Lee. Cancellable Biometrics and Annotations on BioHash. *Pattern Recognition*, 41(6):2034–2044, June 2008. DOI: 10.1016/j.patcog.2007.12.002 Cited on page(s) 24

[163] Andrew B.J. Teoh and David C.L. Ngo. Cancellable Biometerics Featuring with Tokenised Random Number. *Pattern Recognition Letters*, 26(10):1454–1460, July 2005. Cited on page(s) 24

[164] Andrew B.J. Teoh, David C.L. Ngo, and Alwyn Goh. Personalised Cryptographic Key Generation based on Facehashing. *Computers & Security*, 23:606–614, 2004. DOI: 10.1016/j.cose.2004.06.002 Cited on page(s) 46

[165] Achint O. Thomas, Nalini K. Ratha, Jonathan H. Connell, and Ruud M. Bolle. Comparative Analysis of Registration based and Registration Free Methods for Cancelable Fingerprint Biometrics. In *International Conference on Pattern Recognition (ICPR)*, 2008. DOI: 10.1109/ICPR.2008.4761461 Cited on page(s) 25

[166] Valérie Viet Triem Tong, Herv Sibert, Jeremy Lecoeur, and Marc Girault. Biometric Fuzzy Extractors Made Practical: A Proposal based on Fingercodes. In Seong-Whan Lee and Stan Z. Li, editors, *Proceedings of ICB*, pages 604–613, 2007. Cited on page(s) 51

[167] Pim Tuyls, Anton H.M. Akkermans, Tom A.M. Kevenaar, Geert-Jan Schrijen, Asker M. Bazen, and Raymond N.J. Veldhuis. Practical Biometric Authentication with Template Protection. In *Audio- and Video-based Biometric Person Authentication (AVBPA)*, 2005. DOI: 10.1007/11527923_45 Cited on page(s) 50

[168] Pim Tuyls and Jasper Goseling. Capacity and Examples of Template-Protecting Biometric Authentication Systems. In D. Maltoni and Anil K. Jain, editors, *Biometric Authentication Workshop*, 2004. Cited on page(s) 46

[169] Pim Tuyls, Boris Škorić, and Tom Kevenaar, editors. *Security with Noisy Data*. Springer, 2007. Cited on page(s) 97

[170] Yoshifumi Ueshige and Kouichi Sakurai. A Proposal of One-Time Biometric Authentication. In H. R. Arabnia and S. Aissi, editors, *Security and Management*, 2006. Cited on page(s) 81, 83

[171] U. Uludag and A. Jain. Securing Fingerprint Template: Fuzzy Vault with Helper Data. In *Proc. of the 2006 Conference on Computer Vision and Pattern Recognition Workshop*, pages 163–170, June 2006. DOI: 10.1109/CVPRW.2006.185 Cited on page(s) 49

[172] Umut Uludag. *Secure Biometric Systems*. Ph.D. thesis, Michigan State University, 2006. Cited on page(s) 49

[173] Umut Uludag and Anil K. Jain. Fuzzy Fingerprint Vault. In *Proc. Workshop: Biometrics: Challenges Arising from Theory to Practice*, pages 13–16, August 2004. Cited on page(s) 49

[174] Maneesh Upmanyu, Anoop M. Namboodiri, K. Srinathan, and C.V. Jawahar. Efficient Biometric Verification in Encrypted Domain. In *International Conference on Biometrics (ICB)*, 2009. DOI: 10.1007/978-3-642-01793-3_91 Cited on page(s) 82

[175] Maneesh Upmanyu, Anoop M. Namboodiri, Kannan Srinathan, and C. V. Jawahar. Blind Authentication: A Secure Crypto-Biometric Verification Protocol. *IEEE Transactions on Information Forensics and Security*, 5(2):255–268, June 2010. DOI: 10.1109/TIFS.2010.2043188 Cited on page(s) 82, 83

[176] Michiel van der Veen, Tom Kevenaar, Geert-Jan Schrijen, Ton H. Akkermans, and Fei Zuo. Face Biometrics with Renewable Templates. In *Security, Steganography, and Watermarking of Multimedia Contents VIII*, January 2006. DOI: 10.1117/12.643176 Cited on page(s) 50

[177] Claus Vielhauer, Ralf Steinmetz, and Astrid Mayerhöfer. Biometric Hash based on Statistical Features of Online Signatures. In *Proceedings of the 16th International Conference on Pattern Recognition*, 2002. DOI: 10.1109/ICPR.2002.1044628 Cited on page(s) 46

[178] Zhifang Wang, Qi Han, Xiamu Niu, and Christoph Busch. A Novel Template Protection Algorithm for Iris Recognition. In *International Conference on Intelligent Systems Design and Applications (ISDA)*, 2008. DOI: 10.1109/ISDA.2008.202 Cited on page(s) 50

[179] Xiangqian Wu, Ning Qi, Kuanquan Wang, and David Zhang. A Novel Cryptosystem based on Iris Key Generation. In *Fourth International Conference on Natural Computation. (ICNC)*, 2008. DOI: 10.1109/ICNC.2008.808 Cited on page(s) 46

[180] Shenglin Yang and Ingrid Verbauwhede. Automatic Secure Fingerprint Verification System based on Fuzzy Vault Scheme. In *International Conference on Acoustics, Speech, and Signal Processing*, 2005. Cited on page(s) 51

[181] Shenglin Yang and Ingrid Verbauwhede. Secure Iris Verification. In *IEEE International Conference on Acoustics, Speech and Signal Processing (ICASSP-2007)*, volume 2, pages II–133 – II–136, April 2007. DOI: 10.1109/ICASSP.2007.366190 Cited on page(s) 50

[182] Shenglin Yang and Ingrid M. Verbauwhede. Secure Fuzzy Vault based Fingerprint Verification System. In *Thirty-Eighth Asilomar Conference on Signals, Systems and Computers*, 2004. DOI: 10.1109/ACSSC.2004.1399199 Cited on page(s) 51

[183] Gang Zheng, Wanqing Li, and Ce Zhan. Cryptographic Key Generation from Biometric Data using Lattice Mapping. In *ICPR '06: Proceedings of the 18th International Conference on Pattern Recognition*, pages 513–516, Washington, DC, USA, 2006. IEEE Computer Society. DOI: 10.1109/ICPR.2006.423 Cited on page(s) 51

[184] Xuebing Zhou. Template Protection and its Implementation in 3D Face Recognition Systems. *Proceedings of the SPIE*, 6539:65390L, 2007. DOI: 10.1117/12.719845 Cited on page(s) 50

[185] Xuebing Zhou and Christoph Busch. A Novel Privacy Enhancing Algorithm for Biometric System. In *Proceedings of the Special Interest Group on Biometrics and Electronic Signatures*, September 2008. Cited on page(s) 51

[186] Jinyu Zuo, Nalini K. Ratha, and Jonathan H. Connell. Cancelable Iris Biometric. In *International Conference on Pattern Recognition (ICPR)*, 2008. DOI: 10.1109/ICPR.2008.4761886 Cited on page(s) 25

Author's Biography

SANJAY GANESH KANADE

Sanjay Ganesh Kanade obtained his Masters degree in Instrumentation engineering from SGGS Institute of Engineering and Technology, Nanded, India, and a Ph.D. in Computer Science from Institut Télécom SudParis, France, in 2010. His Ph.D. research was in the field of information security by combining biometrics with cryptography, while preserving privacy. At present, he is a post-doctoral researcher at Mines Télécom SudParis. His research interests include signal and image processing, pattern recognition, biometrics, coding theory, and cryptography. As of May 2012, his full list of publications include one patent, one journal paper, and ten publications in conference proceedings.

DIJANA PETROVSKA-DELACRÉTAZ

Dijana Petrovska-Delacrétaz obtained her degree in Physics and Ph.D. from the Swiss Federal Institute of Technology (EPFL) in Lausanne. She was working as a Consultant at AT&T Speech Research Laboratories and as a post-Doc at Télécom ParisTech (for two years), and as a Senior Scientist for four years at the Informatics Department of Fribourg University, Switzerland. She currently holds an assistant professor position within Mines Télécom SudParis. Her research activities are oriented towards pattern recognition, signal processing, and data-driven machine learning methods, that are exploited for different applications such as speech, speaker and language recognition, very low-bit speech compression, biometrics (2D and 3D face, and voice), and crypto-biometrics (including privacy preserving biometrics). As of May 2012, her full list of publications (see also http://webspace.it-sudparis.eu/~petrovs) is composed of three patents, two publicly available databases (for speaker recognition and biometrics evaluations), two collections of open-source software, one book, 19 book chapters and journal papers, and 55 publications in conferences proceedings.

BERNADETTE DORIZZI

Bernadette Dorizzi obtained her Ph.D. (Thèse d'état) in Theoretical Physics at the University of Orsay (Paris XI-France) in 1983, on the study of integrability of dynamical systems. She has been a Professor at Télécom SudParis (ex-INT) since September 1989, and led the Electronics and PHysics (EPH) department from 1995–2009. She is in charge of the Intermedia (Interaction for Multimedia) research team, and her research domain is related to pattern recognition and machine learning applied to activity detection, surveillance-video, and biometrics. She is the coordinator of the Bio-Identity Institut Mines-Télécom research project (`http://biometrics.it-sudparis.eu/english/`) and of the BioSecure Foundation (`http://biosecure.info`). She is the author of more than 300 research papers and has supervised more than 15 Ph.D. theses.

Printed in the United States
by Baker & Taylor Publisher Services